Great is Our God...
and Greatly to Be Praised!

[Memoirs of such an Unworthy Child]

I am not worthy of the least of all the mercies, and of all the truth, which thou hast shewed unto thy servant;
...Genesis 32:101

ConnieJean Harper

Great is our God...and Greatly to Be Praised!

This book is written to provide information and motivation to readers. Its purpose is not to render any type of psychological, legal, or professional advice of any kind. The content is the sole opinion and expression of the author, and not necessarily that of the publisher.

Copyright © 2021 by ConnieJean Harper.

All rights reserved. No part of this book may be reproduced, transmitted, or distributed in any form by any means, including, but not limited to, recording, photocopying, or taking screenshots of parts of the book, without prior written permission from the author or the publisher. Brief quotations for noncommercial purposes, such as book reviews, permitted by Fair Use of the U.S. Copyright Law, are allowed without written permissions, as long as such quotations do not cause damage to the book's commercial value. For permissions, write to the publisher, whose address is stated below.

Printed in the United States of America.

ISBN   978-1-955363-30-3   (Paperback)
ISBN   978-1-955363-31-0   (Digital)

Lettra Press books may be ordered through booksellers or by contacting:

Lettra Press LLC
30 N Gould St. Suite 4753
Sheridan, WY 82801
1 307-200-3414 | info@lettrapress.com
www.lettrapress.com

*"What the Lord Jesus Christ has done
for others he will do for you".
ConnieJean*

CONTENTS

ACKNOWLEDGEMENTS ix
DEDICATION xi
FOREWORD xiii
FOREWORD xv
INTRODUCTION xvii

1. MAURICE'S MIRACLE [Raised From the Dead] 1
2. SONNY'S FIRST CRY [Still Born] 33
3. A DEVASTATING DILEMMA [Mary Helen's] . 43
4. AGAINST ALL ODDS [ConnieJean's Birth] 51
5. 'KABOOSKI' & 'KANEKA' [Sonny & ConnieJean] 63
6. A PRICE WORTH PAYING? [Suffering] 71
7. AND THE MORTARS FELL [Seth - WWII] 79
8. LED BY A CHILD [Danger!] 85
9. '2' ... '4' ... '6 EEE' [As a Little Child] 105
10. JUST KEEP LOVING [Check the Fruit] 119
11. MARY HELEN'S TRIAL [Stomach Cancer] 129
12. HEY, WHAT'D YOU SAY? [ConnieJean Profoundly Deaf] 149
13. THE MOVE IS ON [Mary Helen's Dream] 165
14. ON A QUEST [Elton's Questions] 179
15. A NEW BEGINNING [ConnieJean Remembers] . 185
16. SUMMARY 201

ABOUT THE AUTHOR 205
APPENDIX 207

ACKNOWLEDGEMENTS

Gordon M Harper, Jr.
Rev. David Snodderly
Rev. Mark P. Marquart
Linda Snodderly
Sherry Hartman

- And others
who have edited, shared their time, knowledge, skills
and encouragement to bring this book to its completion

Thank you one and all!

DEDICATION

This book is humbly dedicated to:

Gordon M. Harper, Jr., my husband,

Without his support and love to sustain and encourage me this book could not have been written.

To the descendants of :
David Snider Marquart [1875-1961]
May they truly know the rich heritage they have in our Lord and Savior.

And **to all who read its pages** may the precious Holy Spirit permeate each page revealing the reality of God our Father. May you come to know our Lord's presence and love in a deeper stronger way than you have ever known Him before, may you know our Lord's heart desire is to love you, care for you, and meet your needs, and above all else may His will be done in your lives.

NO ONE – will love you or be your constant companion and friend like our most precious Lord.

ConnieJean Marquart-Harper

FOREWORD

If you are looking for a book that will inspire you to believe that God is a God of miracles, and that Jesus Christ is the same yesterday, today, and forever, and that the God of miracles can be 'your' God for miracles in your own life, then this is the book for you. Not only does ConnieJean share her miraculous life experiences, but she also shares about the God of those miracles; and where in the Word you can find Biblical confirmations.

Do we need to see miracles today? Yes and absolutely! It will be the only way for today's world to know that God is real, and that He can do the same for those who will believe and put their trust in Him. I have known ConnieJean and her husband for quite a few years now. As her Pastor, I can say her integrity and humility is without question. She is an excellent Bible teacher in our church, and truly loves to spend time in its study and with its Author. So follow along as ConnieJean unfolds the truths of God's Word through her family members' experiences. This is a must read for those who are truly searching for the real thing today, and I believe you will become excited as God makes Himself real to you as this powerful story unfolds.

Pastor David Snodderly

Souls Harbor Assembly of God
Auburn, IN 46706

FOREWORD

I am elated to see ConnieJean Harper's book published. ConnieJean is my cousin, Seth, my father, was the brother of Maurice, ConnieJean's father. Dad and Maurice, and our families were very close. We spent a lot of time with each other over the years. I witnessed many miracles while attending the church where Uncle Maurice served as pastor, and I can testify to the authenticity of the miracles ConnieJean has related in the contents of this book.

Growing up the first miracle I remember seeing God perform happened when I was fourteen years old. After that, being the son of a true charismatic Christian, I was privileged and blessed to be in Uncle Maurice's bible believing church. Many times, around an old-fashioned altar, we witnessed God's miracle giving power. Having been a part of this amazing family; I grew up hearing about the power of God and how He had brought back my uncle from the dead after a car accident. How He brought my cousin (ConnieJean's brother) from the dead at birth. How He healed my aunt after Sonny was born. How He healed ConnieJean from being deaf. And so many more amazing and powerful miracles.

These stories are factual, accurate, and told the way they happened. The contents of this book are testimonies to the fact that our God is still in the miracle working business! Th is book should be placed in the hands of anyone who needs God to work a miracle in their life. It will build their faith, encourage them, strengthen, and solidify their resolve to trust God for the answer. ConnieJean has included some excellent nuggets of teaching from God's Word along with their related testimonies. This book will excite you, enlighten you, educate you in the Word of God, and energize your faith to see God move in your life. Once you have finished reading this powerful book, you will want to pass it on to everyone you know who needs a miracle to happen in his or her life.

Pastor Mark Marquart

Independent Full Gospel Church Ashley, IN 46705

INTRODUCTION

In the writing of this book, it is my desire to renew the wonder and awesomeness of our Lord and Savior in your life by recounting, to the best of my recollection, the mighty works of God in the lives of one family. It is my prayer God's precious Holy Spirit accompanies each page of this book and reveals His desire to be your all in all, to bring your faith to a depth you have never experienced before in your lives, for it is written:

Jesus answered and said unto them, Verily I say unto you, If ye have faith, and doubt not, ye shall not only do this which is done to the fig tree, but also if ye shall say unto this mountain, Be thou removed, and be thou cast into the sea; it shall be done. And all things, whatsoever ye shall ask in prayer, believing, ye shall receive. Matthew 21:21-22[2] **Beloved, if our heart condemn us not, then have we confidence toward God. And whatsoever we ask, we receive of him, because we keep his commandments, and do those things that are pleasing in his sight.** 1 John 3:21-22[3] And he said unto them, Go ye into all the world, and preach the gospel to every creature. He that believeth and is baptized shall be saved; but he that believeth not shall be damned. And these signs shall follow them that believe; In my name shall they cast out devils; they shall speak with new tongues; They shall take up serpents; and if they drink any deadly thing, it shall not hurt them; they shall lay hands on the sick, and they **shall recover. And they went forth, and preached everywhere, the Lord working with them, and confirming the word with signs following. Amen.** Mark 16:15-18, 20[4] **Doubt not, for the events you are about to hear are true. Let your heart be fed by 'His Word' and guided by 'His Spirit' as you read; reach out and claim all He has prepared for you. For there is no respect of persons with God.** Romans 2:11[5] Jesus Christ the same yesterday, and to day, and for ever. Hebrews 13:8[6]

What He has done for others
He will do for you!

ConnieJean

DAVID SNIDER MARQUART

ISAAC IMES MARQUART

MAURICE ERVIN MARQUART

MARY HELEN PIERCE-MARQUART

The Miracle Family

1838 - 1953

MAURICE LEROY MARQUART

CONNIEJEAN MARQUART

MAURICE'S MIRACLE
[Raised From the Dead]
1

How about grabbing a cup of coffee and coming over here to sit and chat for a while - if you're not too busy. I really would like to talk with you about something that has been on my mind for some time.

There's a yellow cup in the cabinet on the right side of the sink, the middle shelf - yeah, that's the one. The coffee is on the counter in the corner next to the appliance garage, no silly, not the garage, the appliance garage on the counter!

Sit here on the lounge chair next to me. All comfy?

I've had something on my mind for some time and was wondering, do you ever wonder, "where are the miracles and wonders of God these days?"

Right, I know it is a serious religious question, but have you? I really would like to know. I have wondered so many times. I keep thinking, what does it take to have a miracle and to see God's wondrous works in our day and age. Are there any stepby-step instructions, "this way to a miracle?" Everyone wants to experience and see miracles; I do, don't you? We long to see them with our own eyes. I've heard people say, "If I could just see a miracle, experience the wonder of God, it'd make all the difference in the world; why, I'd never fall or backslide! I'd be so strong, so on fire for God!" I keep thinking, we need that kind of demonstration of God's power today, in our day and time. But, what does it take to have a miracle? Do you know?

Have you ever experienced it yourself? Have you ever known anyone who has actually experienced a "real" miracle of God?

No?

Most folks I know today not only have not received a miracle, they haven't even seen a real honest-to-goodness miracle and don't personally know anyone who has!

But I know a family who grew up and spent their early years in a small farm town in the state of Indiana, a family who received many wonders and miracles from our Lord. They weren't really important to anyone but their own kin and friends, maybe a handful of others they had become acquainted with as they grew up and had their own families, but I was told those people who knew them in the 1940's called them "the miracle family". As most families in small farm towns in those days, they were very poor, just a family - a father, mother, son, and daughter - struggling to get by. Truth be known, their lives and struggles were greater than most, even in those days. On the surface, they just seemed like common folks, no different than you and me. Guess what, they were just like your mother and father, the neighbors next door, or the family on the other side of town - just like you and me. They were just plain, everyday folks.

I can tell you what I heard and know if you would like to hear about them.

You would.

Okay. Well, Maurice, the father, was born on January 4, 1917, in the small town of Monroeville, to Dave and Cora. I really do not know a whole lot about Dave and Cora's parents, except to say Dave was the fifth of seven children born to Isaac and Martha. Maurice's grandfather, Isaac, was one of a set of triplet boys born in 1837 and later he became known as "an old Allen County pioneer" - one of the oldest and most prominent settlers of Madison township.

Isaac enlisted in the thirtieth Indiana volunteer infantry at the age of twenty-four, and after he returned to Madison township, became known as one of the great hunters of the country. He hunted the hunting grounds of Maine as well as other known hunting states. It is said that at the young age of seventy-one, he joined a hunting party and spent part of a winter hunting big game in Wisconsin; and as a marksman, he had no known rival. When there were marksman competitions, often the sign would say something like, "All are welcome, except Isaac Marquart." No one would pay the entrance fee if Isaac's name was on the list of competitors.

At the age of thirty-three, Isaac joined the German Baptist church, and it was said he was a faithful member until his death; he served several years as a deacon of the church. While Isaac was in Georgia during the Civil War, he was inspired by memorials seen there to sketch his own memorial. After returning home after the war, Isaac had the memorial carved and it still stands proud today in the Monroeville Memorial Cemetery with a cement replica of his beloved hunting rifle on the stone base and the flame of liberty on the left of the face of the stone.

Isaac (1838-1913) & Martha (Clear/1840-1926) Marquart

I'm really sorry to say I know very little about his wife, Martha, except to say their union gave birth to seven children - five boys and two girls. The fifth child born to Isaac and Martha was a strapping boy they named David [Dave].

Dave grew up as a next-door neighbor to a sweet little girl named Cora Snider; the families were so close Dave's parents gave him Cora's maiden name, Snider, for his middle name. Hmm, I believe I smell a little plot brewing.

I'm telling you all this family information so we can try to figure out if Maurice and Mary Helen's upbringing or heritage might have had anything to do with them receiving all those miracles from God.

Oh, so you'd like to hear more about them? Okay. Good.

Great is Our God... and Greatly to Be Praised!

David (1875-1961) & Cora (Snider/1881-1959) Marquart

Well, I don't know exactly how this happened, but Dave, the son of a German Baptist, became a Methodist and married the sweet, little Catholic girl next door, Cora. And, the faithful German Baptist's funeral was held in the United Brethren church, which makes me wonder if Martha was not of the German Baptist belief, but of the United Brethren. Maybe Isaac's church spoke German and Martha didn't. But, do you see where I am going with this? This "miracle family" appears to have come out of a religious mutt heritage; you know, sort of like the old Heinz 57 Varieties version. This little, seemingly unimportant fact gives us something to ponder - are wonders and miracles the property or gift of only a certain few or a particular church or denomination? Could it be all in the purpose and plan of our Maker to bring forth a demonstration of His power and love on a family of such diverse church affiliations? Is it possible He, our Lord and our God, was trying to show us it is not the denomination or the building you attend, but it's the God you worship and serve and how you seek Him that matters. I looked up some Scripture. Here, let me read them to you.

"But if from thence *thou shalt seek the Lord thy God,* thou shalt find him, if thou seek him *with all thy heart and with all thy soul.*" Deuteronomy 4:29[7] "Only fear the Lord, and *serve him in truth with all your heart:* for consider how great things he hath done for you." 1 Samuel 12:24[8] "*...thou shalt find Him.*" (Now go back and read just the italicized portions of those scriptures.)

These Scriptures tell me it's God, and only God, that matters here. Sure, some churches are definitely more encouraging and seem to believe more strongly in miracles and healing, but to me, these Scriptures are saying, "It's all up to you." Receiving miracles and healing does not depend on which church you belong to or the denomination you are affiliated with; it's your desire to seek the truth, to seek God and to serve Him with all your heart and soul.

Is it possible this is one of the steps, a clue to receiving signs and wonders, miracles from our Lord? Seek the Lord with all your heart and soul, and fear the Lord your God and serve Him in truth with all your heart.

Okay, wait a minute; I'm getting ahead of myself here. I'd really like you to come to know Maurice's father, Dave. He was a big part of a couple of the miracles I am going to tell you, so maybe we can find some answers in knowing him a little bit better.

I was told that as a young man, Dave worked on the railroad, and I was shown a picture of Dave and his crew. The story goes that one day he was assigned as the crew leader, but that did not go down very well with others on the crew. I believe they said he had not been part of this crew as long as some of the other workers. Anyway, I figure Dave must have been a very strong man. It seems he came up with a peaceful way to settle the dispute. He said they would each in turn throw a railroad spike at the rail car some distance away and the person who proved to be the strongest by throwing their spike the furthest would be the new crew leader. Hmm, I'm wondering what the man in charge would have thought of this arrangement, had he known. You know, the boss. Anyway, all agreed, each man thinking he was stronger than Dave and could possibly win this contest and become the new crew leader. Each in turn took his spike and threw it at the rail car with all his might. The spikes lay on the ground at various distances from the rail car; some much closer than others.

Then Dave stepped up and picked up his spike. He threw it with all his might, and it hurled through the air towards the rail car. All the men stood in silence and unbelief as they witnessed Dave's spike stuck in the side of that rail car. It was said there was never a question after that incident as to whom the strongest person was on that crew, or who would be their crew leader.

Later in life, I'm told, Dave was well known in town, as he co-owned the Mercantile. A Mercantile was like a baby Super Wal-Mart; it had a little bit of everything most needed by the local folks, but not a whole lot of any one thing - especially in those days. This is the store where all the town folks would go for their food supplies, clothes, school supplies, pots and pans, and hardware. Why, one could even find those wonderful little penny candies in ole Dave's store. But even greater than all those things, everyone could find a genuine neighbor and friend in dear ole Dave.

I never heard when or what the circumstances were that led to Dave's spiritual conversion, or how old he was when he made his decision to accept and serve our Lord. But I was told he was a Christian who lived what he believed at all times, one who the entire town knew would say he would pray for them and their needs - and he really honestly did! Although Dave was known for being a small businessman in town, to his family he had an even more impressive title. He was known as the town's "official unofficial pastor." Everyone came to ole Dave when they wanted someone to pray for them, or about their needs. You did not have to belong to any special church or hold to the same doctrines as he did. All you needed to do was ask him to pray. [They said when Dave passed away, a member of his family found an ole spiral notebook full of names - his prayer list. It was said that Dave prayed for every name in that book every day of his life. Once your name was entered into Dave's book, you were in there for life.]

There is so much more to tell you about Dave, but we will come to more of his story later. I will tell you this, Dave was a Bible believer. If the Bible said it, then that is what he believed and how he tried to live his life.

One time Dave was asked why he almost always had a cup of water in his hands. I was told he told of an incident when he was talking to a man in town that was known to drink too much, and trying to persuade him of the wrong and harm of drinking to excess. Dave tried to explain what the Word of God had to say about his situation.[9] He was said to have tried to explain how really hard the times were and it was hard to feed and care for a family in these times, it was money needed to meet his family's needs, not wants, that he was drinking. The man is said to have looked at Dave for a minute or two and then asked, "Dave, are the times hard for you? Is it hard for you to meet the needs of your big family of eleven? I never see you without a cup of coffee in your hands. How is that different? You are drinking up money that could be used to meet the needs of your family. Why, you're just as much "needy" of that cup of coffee as I am my alcohol!"

Dave *never* drank another cup of coffee. His cup of coffee was not worth a soul or causing the stumbling of his neighbor or friend; besides, the man was right. That money, no matter how little, could be spent on needs. After that day, you would still see Dave walking around town or in his Mercantile with a cup in his hand, a cup of water.

My, what determination to care for the needs of others before your own. Just think what this world would be like if all God's children would live this kind of life! If we could only understand, everyone is better off when we think of others before ourselves. Can you just imagine what life would be like? Why, it would be like heaven on earth with everyone more concerned with the needs and desires of the other person and not themselves. The devil has so blinded our eyes and minds with all this "my rights, my space, my way" stuff. Me, me, me! In our world today, our young people are bombarded with teachers, guidance counselors, psychologists, movie stars, and yes, even some get-rich-quick ministers telling them it's all about them and what "they" want.

But, isn't that what Satan told Eve in the garden?[10] Just eat of the forbidden fruit and you can be like God; you can know everything. In our day and age, knowledge is king. We are led to believe knowledge will get us everything our little heart's desire. We are seeking the knowledge of the world, the universe, and forgetting the soul within, which is starving and withering from neglect. Can you just imagine what it would be like if everyone was working hard, trying to do and give the most to others? I really think this could be an important clue/key to receiving miracles from God. The Bible says "... take heed lest by any means this liberty of yours become a stumbling block to them that are weak." 1 Corinthians. 8:9[11] "Let us not therefore judge one another any more: but judge this rather, that no man put a stumbling block or an occasion to fall in his brother's way." Romans. 14:13[12] and "He that loveth his brother abideth in the light, and there is none occasion of stumbling in him" 1 John 2:10[13]

These Scriptures tell me there is a definite link between how much I care for the needs of my brother - my concern for his walk in the Lord, to the extent I will not fulfill my personal wants if it will hinder his walk and abiding in the light. Who is our "light"? Is it not Christ Jesus![14] If we are to walk fully in the light, we must be willing to take up our cross and follow.

Jesus has said in His Word ". . . he that taketh not his cross, and followeth after me, is not worthy of me. He that findeth his life shall lose it: and he that loseth his life for my sake shall find it." Matthew 10:38-39[15] Just as our Savior was willing to pay the ultimate price and take up His cross that we may have life, the light of life, we are called to take up our crosses and surrender to a life of serving others.

He, our Lord and our Savior, is our example. It is in His likeness and image we are to walk and have our being. "For in him we live, and move, and have our being..." Acts 17:28[16] When he humbled himself to wash the feet of his disciples, he said "For I have given you an example, that ye should do as I have done to you." John 13:15[17] Was our Lord talking only about literally washing one another's feet in a ceremony? No, he was telling us we are called to be servants of our brothers and sisters; we are called to take on the position of caring for the needs of others.

Okay, so what have we discovered in the lives of this miracle family so far?

1. Seek the Lord with all your heart and soul, and fear the Lord your God and serve Him in truth with all your heart.
2. It isn't the denomination or the building you attend; it's the God you worship and serve and how you seek Him that matters.
3. Be a genuine neighbor and friend.
4. Be a faithful prayer warrior on the behalf of others.
5. Care for and have concern for the needs of others <u>above your own</u> wants and desires.

Let's see, where were we? Oh, would you like to hear a little love story?

Okay, well exactly six months to the day, on July 4th, 1917, Cora dressed her new little boy [Maurice] and left their home on Lincoln Street going southwest about the distance of two or three houses. They then turned south down West Barnhart Street to see the new baby girl born a few houses down the street to Earl and Mary. Oh, by the way, Earl and Mary taught Sunday School in the Evangelical United Brethren church in town.

Cora took one look at that beautiful little girl and said, "I would like her to be my daughter someday." I heard nothing about their families socializing or doing anything together. I don't really know if the two little ones ever really knew each other; but they sure did later!

Maurice grew to be a terribly shy little boy. So shy, he would run and hide under the bed or in a closet if anyone came into their house, and there he'd stay until everyone - even aunts, uncles, and cousins - had left the house. However, that would change. Someone was to come along and pierce that fortress he had so successfully built around himself. Just guess who 'she' was.

Maurice and Mary Helen told the story themselves. On the first day of school, the teacher took her class to the gymnasium for their gym class, and then asked them all to find a "buddy" for the day's activities. Both Maurice and Mary Helen, on opposite sides of the gym, looked around the gym. When they saw each other, they ran across the gym floor to be buddies. They were married in spirit from that day on; they always did everything together. The beautiful little girl took the shy little boy under her wing to encourage and help him all along the way. Maurice often said he would probably never have gotten through school if it had not been for his Mary Helen.

Later in high school, Maurice would spend hours and hours in an empty gym alone practicing to "make hoops" so he could join the basketball team and impress the now-very-popular young lady. He made the team, which then went on to win the state championship for their town and little school. As I heard it told, at one point during their high school years,

Great is Our God... and Greatly to Be Praised!

Earl (1892-1960) & Mary Louise (Stevens/1895-1961) Piercew

it was decided they should date someone else [hmm, my guess would be by the outgoing and very popular Mary Helen]. They went out on a double date, each with another person, but together in the same car and going to the same event. It seems they couldn't even do that without the other one nearby! Before the date was over, Maurice and Mary Helen were back arm-in-arm and, to my knowledge, that was the last, and only time, they dated anyone else. As I said, this couple did everything together. By the time they became seniors, there had been a change in Maurice. Although still shy, he was able to become the male lead in the senior play along-side Mary Helen as the female lead; he could do anything with her at his side.

There's more. Do you want to hear more about Dave?

Maurice E. Marquart (1917-2002) & Mary Helen Pierce (1917-2002), Monroeville, Indiana, Senior Class Play Photograph.

Okay, a short one - just to help you understand this man called Dave, Maurice's father, and one of his lessons/influences on his son.

It seems Dave was not the best of businessmen, but he was the best of friends. One of the stories I was told is that, no matter what the circumstance, he never, ever turned anyone away when they came into his store in need of food or supplies. His customer's bill could be more than the customer could possibly pay in months and months of labor, but he wouldn't be turned away. In fact, many of the balances were beyond a near future pay-off date, as these were war days and everyone was struggling just to survive.

Maurice learned a lesson in that store one day that he would never forget. When Maurice was a teenager, Dave injured one of his legs or feet quite badly, can't remember which, and Maurice was given the responsibility to help mind the store until Dave could once again go back to work. I can just imagine a restless teenager meandering around the store aimlessly when there were no customers, and, as all teenagers seem to do, thinking he was quite smart. Of course, he only meant to help his father, but at some point, he ended up looking through the books and seeing that all their neighbors owed them a lot of money. Maybe he even thought of a thing or two he wanted, but was told the family could not afford to get it for him. Maybe it made him feel important and a little powerful, I don't know, but whatever his reason or motive, Maurice took postcards and began making out bills he would send to all those people who "owed them" money.

After ole Dave was well enough to go back to work, people - his neighbors - came into his store one by one to explain why they had not paid their bill and gave him the few coins they had in their pockets. It was said in some incidents Dave refused to accept their payment, as he knew they had greater needs than paying that bill. Dave always believed in, and trusted, his neighbors and friends; come to think of it, he trusted everyone. His set pat rule was "These are good folks; they would not put it on a bill if they had the money to buy it. When they have the money, they will pay their bill." [Oh, if only we could learn to live like Dave believed people to be today in our credit card society. Might I add here another word of wisdom I heard over the years, "if you can't afford it, don't have the money to buy it, DON'T." The truth is, we don't "need" all that stuff we put ourselves in bondage for to pay off later, not to mention all the additional interest it accumulates.]

Whoops digressed there a bit; back to Maurice's lesson.

Maurice was called on the carpet and asked why in the world he embarrassed their friends and neighbors like that, calling them to task for something beyond their ability to do at this time! If any one of them would have had the money to do so, they would have paid for all their food and supplies. They did not need him [Maurice] to tell them what they owed and couldn't pay! God has met our needs and always put food on our table, we don't need to take money from people who will go cold or without milk for their children. God provides!

Maurice was then required, in one way or another, to contact everyone he had sent a dun and tell them it was a mistake. He had written and sent out the bills without his father's knowledge or consent. They were to "ignore the bill" and, Dave said, "not to worry about it." He knew they had more pressing needs and would pay the store when they had the money to do so. [Among other things, this sounds like a good lesson in respecting and obeying those in authority over you, even when you think you have a better idea or can do something better your way.]

Another book, a ledger, was found after Dave had gone to be with the Lord. The ledger had all the names of people who had received food and supplies during those war years. When the store closed, Dave considered all the debts closed, too. I was told he did not see this as being gypped or done out of what was owed him, but in his heart, he thanked our good Lord for making it possible for him to help all those people during their hard times. For God's word says ". . . Verily I say unto you, Inasmuch as ye have done it unto one of the least of these my brethren, ye have done it unto me." Matthew 25:40[18]

Th rough it all, his family did not go without even one single un-met need by our Lord.

Wouldn't it be something if we could all learn God pays, gives, more than we give away to others. We have less when we give less, when we do less for others. The tighter we hold on to what we have, the less that will flow back to us. Do you remember the parable of the talents in the bible?[19] It was the servant who did the most with what he had been given who received the greatest reward, not the servant who held on tight and buried it. All that we have has come from God and it is His desire that we, as His stewards, should share it with others. Don't be afraid, you won't run out, not as long as you give it with a pure heart as unto God. God is a giver! He wants His children to be like Him, giving to those around us who are in need. "...God, that giveth to all men liberally..." James 1:5[20] "...God, who giveth us richly all things to enjoy" 1 Timothy 6:17[21] We are instructed in His precious Word to us to care, to do, and to give: when we do for others, we are doing for our Lord and Savior.[22]

If we do not have works along with our faith, our faith is dead. James 2:14-17[23] tells us our faith is unprofitable and dead if we do not meet the needs of others.

At this point, I must tell you I am not absolutely certain as to the chronological order of these following events, they were told to me at different times, and no clear picture of a time line was given.

There are only two incidents, Maurice's miracle and salvation, which one might feel the order of the events might be important, but I do not. Our precious Jesus healed both the follower and the sinner when He walked this earth. I will try to relate the events in order as best I can.

Maurice was told by a friend that he was sure he would be hired if he came to Pontiac, Michigan and applied for a position with the company where he worked. I believe this company may have been the Pontiac Motor Co., a division of General Motors. As the story goes, the company had a basketball team and needed some good players. Maurice was hired due to his skill on the basketball floor, not his knowledge of running any presses or machinery.

While Maurice worked in Pontiac, Mary Helen went to Pontiac looking for work and stayed with family members; she became a local drug store employee and, of course, they continued seeing each other.

On the twenty-seventh of December, 1936 Maurice had gotten home for Christmas before Mary Helen. He made arrangements with their minister, and met her at the bus when she arrived. Mary Helen accepted his unexpected proposal of marriage and they went immediately to the minister's home to be married. Mr. and Mrs. went back to Pontiac and found a little apartment. Mary Helen talked of a beautiful little girl living in another apartment, a blue-eyed dark haired little girl who stole her heart. Oh, how she would like a little blue-eyed dark-haired girl of her own someday, but children would have to wait until they were settled and life was easier.

As I recall, they did not go on a honeymoon right away; they both continued working. When the time came, and they went on a belated honeymoon, it was up to Niagara Falls. Maurice had just bought a car, and they would give it a good try-out through Canada and over to Niagara Falls for their honeymoon trip. When they arrived at the border, it seems their new car's paperwork was not all in order. Either something wasn't signed properly, or a paper was missing, I can't really remember what was wrong. But, after their long story of this being their honeymoon and Mary Helen's winning ways, they were given permission to go through to Niagara Falls, with instructions that they would be searched for and found if they did not return through that gate on or before the date they gave for their return date.

Whew, that was a close one! But they were finally off on their weekend honeymoon. In those days, it was not all commercialized and they pulled up under the mist of the falls; sleeping in their new car. In the morning, when no one was around, they would wash off, fully clothed, standing beside the car in the mist of the falls. Oh, by the way, they made it back through that border gate in time after a wonderful time in the mist and beauty of those magnificent falls – a wondrous gift of our precious Lord. How they longed to stay wrapped in its peaceful mist.

One of the stories Mary Helen told, with a mischievous twinkle in her eye, was how she learned to drive by taking their new car out while Maurice was working, and driving up and down the alleys and back streets of Pontiac. When she felt she had her skill honed, Mary Helen showed up to pick Maurice up one night after work, much to his surprise.

I remember hearing about a big labor union strike that took place while Maurice was working in Pontiac, which became very nasty. The employees were locked in so production could continue, and the employees would sustain fewer injuries. Maurice told how they - I don't know who the other men were - crawled out and down an air shaft or heat duct to a nearby building across the road to get out of the building. To my knowledge, that was the end of both his automotive and basketball careers.

It is my impression this is about the time they moved back home to the little town of Monroeville and bought a little house on Monroe Street, across from the school playground and ball diamond. The little home had four rooms downstairs, entering the front door, and walking counter clockwise from room to room around a circled path; there was a front room, dining room with a potbellied stove on a slightly raised platform, kitchen, and bedroom. Two bedrooms were located upstairs dividing the length of the home in half, with a front window overlooking the playground across the street and a back window looking over the back yard, and a small shed and outhouse nestled along the back property line near the alley dividing it from the property facing Summit Street.

God's word says "Train up a child in the way he should go: and when he is old, he will not depart from it." Proverbs 22:6[24] Maurice had most certainly been trained as a child, but Maurice wasn't living for the Lord like he'd been instructed by his father and guided by his mother, trained as a child. As many a wayward child, he was wondering through life doing his own thing and tasting of the world's table, which was conveniently laid out before him by the enemy of his soul. Remember the fruit of the tree of knowledge offered to Eve? "And when the woman saw that the tree was good for food, and that it was pleasant to the eyes, and a tree to be desired to make one wise, she took of the fruit thereof, and did eat, and gave also unto her husband with her; and he did eat." Genesis 3:6[25] Satan's offerings to us will be things we too can reason will be good for . . ., pleasant to our eyes, or things to be desired by our natural flesh. His offerings will always be things we secretly have not totally surrendered to the Lord, things that entice and beckon us.

Maurice either purchased, or won, a pool hall in town on the Northwest corner of Ohio Street and West South Street, I believe; and the games began. His little pool and poker hall became a hopping place with farmers and men of all ages and income levels coming in to see if Lady Luck would be on their side. However, Lady Luck had taken a liking to Maurice and hung on his every shot or turn of a card. Can't you just see Satan gleefully whispering in Maurice's ear, "You're a natural, you just can't lose. It's not your fault if they come in here. They are going to lose their money anyway, why shouldn't you get it?"

Yes, the pool hall was also a place to wager your meager income from long hours of hard work against the cunning hands and mind of Lady Luck's main squeeze. At the end of the day, Maurice would go home from his day's work with the rent, grocery, or bill-paying money of most of those who had wandered into his establishment. Each one hoping to extend their pennies, nickels, and dimes somehow to cover everything their family needed. Instead, they walked away dejected and penniless, more in need, caught in the never ending cycle of the enemy's false promises and dangling hopes. However, for the wives of those men, there was a beautiful lady who seemed like an angel sent straight from God; Mary Helen. Some way, somehow, I never heard how or when, this beautiful lady found out who had lost their bill-paying money and the money that took milk out of the mouths of their kids, so to speak. She would then take the money, which had been lost the night before, and give it to the wives to feed their children and pay their bills.

I cannot tell you how long this cycle of good and evil played out, but one day Maurice was sitting in the little restaurant where Mary Helen worked, talking with a man while he had a bite to eat. The man was saying, "I wish I had a pool hall like yours", and Maurice asked, "Do you really want a pool hall?" The man replied he did, and Maurice asked him, "How much money do you have on you?" It was said the man dug in his pockets and gathered up all the money he had. Maurice said, "If you really want a pool hall, I'll sell it to you for what you hold in your hands." That day the pool hall and everything in it sold for what that man had in his pockets, and Maurice just walked away from the pool hall and that way of life.

Do you know what I was just thinking? Did you notice the cycle of good, bad, and good, during this time in the lives of Dave, Maurice, and Mary Helen? Dave putting the needs of his customers before his own wants and needs, helping his neighbors and friends just survive these war years; while at the same time Maurice, his son, about a half block away from the Mercantile was taking all their hard-earned money in games of chance. Could a loving father have been more crushed, watching his son living in sin and hurting his neighbors and friends – not to mention the bills that could not be paid because the money had been lost to his son. How his heavy heart must have cried out to the Lord in the night for the soul of his son. I can just imagine the effect Mary Helen's gracious heart had on his weeping spirit, knowing she was giving back to those who had lost so much. How gracious our God is! God through Dave 'gave' –The devil's sly lies and influence caused

Maurice to 'take' – but God through Mary Helen 'returned' all they had lost. God will supply our needs! Our God will defeat the plans and deeds of the devil; He will be victorious!

Now I'm guessing it was sometime around this time when Mary Helen had been out one evening and, upon returning home, Maurice took one look at her as she entered their modest little home and asked, "Where have you been, what did you do?" Mary Helen stood there for a minute or two, and then said, "I've been to church." Maurice again asked, "What did you do?" Mary Helen replied, "I went to the altar and got saved." Maurice stood there for a while, I never heard for how long or if anything else was said between the two of them, then he said, "If it's good enough for you, then it's good enough for me, too," he went right upstairs and knelt beside the bed. There, in the privacy of his own home, Maurice asked our Lord, the King of kings, to forgive him of all his sins and for rejecting Him, and to come into his heart, to abide with him forever. Now they were together as they had always been; but now they were together in Him, Christ, our Lord and our Savior. Talk about miracles, this was the greatest miracle of all, the grand-daddy of all miracles they would come to experience in their lives!

All his childhood training, all the prayers of his godly father and mother had been answered, their commitment and faith rewarded.

"GREAT is our GOD, and GREATLY to be PRAISED!

I don't know how long it had been since Maurice and Mary Helen came to accept the Lord in their hearts and lives. I believe Maurice was working in Fort Wayne, Indiana and Mary Helen worked in the same little restaurant in Monroeville when God blessed them with a miracle. It is my feeling our Lord started His work in their lives with the daddy of all miracles: the most colossal event.

The story goes that when the sons of Dave were in their twenty's, a couple were drawn into local politics. Elton, the fourth child of Dave and Cora and nine years older than Maurice, made his career in the political arena for the rest of his life. Dave's family had become sort of important in Monroeville in those days for two reasons; first because of Dave's standing in the community and being a co-owner of the town Mercantile, and second, because of Elton's rapid popularity in the politics of the town. Maurice had tinkered around in the local politics, but it did not seem to be his cup of tea, so to speak, so he got a job out of town, in Fort Wayne, Indiana.

I cannot tell you what time of day or night it was, the day of the week, or the month and year Maurice was driving home from work, but I believe I could still locate the intersection outside of Monroeville. Sirens pierced the air as emergency responders and police rushed out to where two vehicles were broken and mangled. Maurice was pronounced dead on the scene, with his head severed from his body except for a couple of inches of flesh holding it on. His face was torn where the windshield had cut the flesh from his cheek and cut off part of one ear. His head had gone through the windshield, and then pulled back through it again by the force of his car coming to a sudden stop. They were said to have removed his body from the car, laid him on a board with his head in a downward position and tightly nestled against his body, his feet raised, so they could keep his upper body warm long enough to be seen by his father and identified. Then they rushed to attend the other victim. It was said it was impossible for Maurice to have much, if any, blood in him judging by the pool of blood that stained the road and soaked into the soil.

They took Maurice to a nearby hospital to sew him back together before his father would view and identify his son's body. Although Maurice didn't seem to grow cold as quickly as others had following death, the hospital personnel worked as fast as they could to sew his head back onto his body before rigor mortis set in. Since the mortician did not need them to be intact, there was no need to reattach the arteries, muscles, or ligaments, making their surface sewing much faster. Everything appeared to be going pretty well, they only had to reattach the flesh cut out of his face by the windshield and they'd be done. They couldn't reattach the top of his left ear as it wasn't brought in with his body. As they finished sewing Maurice's head back onto his body, Maurice suddenly opened his eyes and asked, "Where am I? What happened?"

Maurice told how everyone seemed to be thrown back against the walls, faces white and mouths hanging open, staring at him. He said they very slowly stepped up to where he was lying, staring at him the whole time as if they were afraid to take their eyes off of him. As they stared at him, Maurice said, "I want to see," but they began trying to convince him it wasn't good for him to see what he looked like right now. After much persistence, one of the doctors handed Maurice a mirror. His face was not all sewn back together yet, but it didn't seem to upset him. He handed the mirror back and they proceeded to sew his face back together. In the meantime, the town reporter was turning in an article on Maurice's accident and death to the Monroeville News. Upon hearing of his coming to life, he pulled the article and later gave Maurice a copy of his original death notice.

When the family and Mary Helen were allowed to see him, the doctor took them aside and told Mary Helen, "He isn't really alive, he can't be, this is something we can't explain." After some time passed, and he was going to be released from the hospital, they told the family again, "He really isn't alive. He will be sitting in a chair or lying in bed and suddenly be gone; there is no way he can truly be alive."

I was not told this, but can you just imagine what Mary Helen and the family went through? Afraid to leave the room for fear he would die while they were in another room. Watching him as he slept to make sure he did not die alone in the night. What a mental and emotional torment that must have been!

I'm sorry to say that I can't remember how long, but after a little time had passed and Maurice still hadn't "finished dying", the doctors told the family, "If his nerves ever reconnect and heal, he will feel all the pain from the accident all at once, it will kill him on the spot. His heart will never be able to take the intense pain he will feel."

Some time passed, I don't know how long. Enough time had passed that life was somewhat back to normal and someone was not watching his every move, when one day Maurice went out to the outhouse. The routine calm of this quiet little farm town was split wide open by the blood curdling screams coming from the outhouse. The screaming, the pounding; it seemed as though he had been locked in with a monster which was ravaging him!

People came running from all directions; neighbors, and friends. Everyone thinking this was it, this time the doctors got it right, Maurice was going to die in horrible pain! But, Maurice did not die, although I am sure there were times he wished he had. Well, at least I am sure I would have rather died than suffer all that excruciating pain. God had other plans for Maurice's life; He had plans Maurice had not fulfilled yet. Treatments followed to reduce the pain until the nerves, muscles, ligaments, etc., all came back together again, and the pain subsided and stopped.

Did this really happen? Can it possibly be true? YES, it really happened!

"*GREAT is our GOD*, and GREATLY to be PRAISED"!

And this was only the beginning of what God had in store for this "miracle family".

Before we go on with their story, did you catch what went before the miracle? They were living a life of service, and caring for the needs of others before their own, suffering pain and hardship, almost beyond endurance, not to mention financial debts that appeared impossible to pay off in a lifetime. Yet, I am told they almost always took in someone in need, to give them shelter, and care for them, and yes, to share their meager food supply with them, too.

Maurice and Mary Helen's life changed, changed for eternity. Their lives became about others even during their darkest hours – always ready to 'do', 'give', 'help' others, and often shared their meager little home and supplies with those in need. In fact, it was said, prior to the 1960's they always made room in their hearts and home for someone needing a place to live or the care of a godly angel of mercy.

I wonder, are we willing to pay the price it takes to receive the great miracles of God and keep caring for others, giving to others, meeting their needs? I remember hearing stories how, at times, things became so rough there was no money to even buy enough to make a simple pot of soup. But everyone - parents, aunts, uncles, cousins, - would get together and each took the few pennies, nickels, dimes, and sometimes a rare quarter they had and put it all together to be able to buy a pound of hamburger for a pot of soup. One would bring a potato or two, another a few carrots, whatever they could find in their bare cupboards, to add to the pot of soup. They found in those days of want, there would be enough to bring a struggling neighbor or friend in to eat if one just added a little more water. But those were also the days of true love one for another, laughter, and singing as they sat around enjoying one another's company and the warmth of a sharing heart. Deeds done from the depth of one's heart always built the warmest fires for family, friends, neighbors, and even strangers to bask in together; to ward off the cold chill of hard times and doing without.

There are times in the quiet of the night I wonder, where has all that caring and sharing gone in the seasons of plenty? Have those heart fires gone down? Are the flames barely flickering since we now can make it on our own and don't need any help? Do we add "just a little water" and feed our less blessed neighbors, friends, and strangers? Are we bringing them into our inner circle of family and friends, where the lonely can become part of us?

What is that scripture? . . . "He that loveth his brother abideth in the light, and there is none occasion of stumbling in him." 1 John 2:10[26] and ". . . Verily I say unto you, Inasmuch as ye have done it unto one of the least of these my brethren, ye have done it unto me." Matthew 25:40[27] and ". . . Even so faith, if it hath not works, is dead, being alone." James 2:17[28]

Is it possible the hard times that have begun to drift across our country, our nation, is to teach us once again "do unto the least of these my brethren"? Will they cause us to once again build those fires of love and care for one another, - to "add a little water" and take strangers into our home, - to feed the hungry, and clothe the naked? Is it really necessary for our Lord and our God to withdraw His hand of protection and blessing upon America as He did His chosen people[29] so we, too, will turn back to our Lord with our whole heart and mind and live serving others as He lived for us? Do you hear the songs of joy, even in the "hard times", and the laughter of a glad heart when you lift your windows at night to let in the cool breezes blowing across our land? What happened to the times of neighbors sitting together around a bon-fire, singing and laughing?

Maybe our steps/clues from the lives of Dave, Maurice and Mary Helen, will be a light to brighten our paths to the way back to God's way, the Bible way, of living for Him. So, what are those clues now

1. Seek the Lord with all your heart and soul, fear the Lord your God and serve Him in truth with all your heart.
2. It isn't the denomination or the building you attend, it's the God you worship and serve and how you seek Him that matters.
3. Be a genuine neighbor and friend.
4. Be a faithful prayer warrior on the behalf of others.
5. Care and have concern for the needs of others above your own wants and desires.
6. Feed the hungry, give drink to the thirsty, take in the stranger, clothe the naked, visit the sick and those in prison.
7. Endure hardships, pain, and/or suffering while maintaining a deep heart-love for others and their needs, even in the time of want.

Well, I don't know about you... But this lady has a lot of room for improvement!

Hey, how's that coffee holding up, ready for a warm up?

Let's stretch our legs a bit and refresh our coffee. The sun is shining outside and there appears to be a gentle breeze blowing, how about going out on the warm deck in the shade if you'd like to hear more about this family?

Are you sure you have the time to spare today?

Wow, doesn't it feel great out here? Just think, our God gave us all this. He even knew what would make us happy, and desired to give us the gift of all our senses so we could enjoy His creation to the fullest. *What a loving God we serve!*

Okay, if you're sure you want to hear more, let's sit out here in the beautiful breeze, the sun's outshining itself today. Smell the wonderful scent of roses drifting across the yard. You know, I don't think I will ever get tired of thanking our God for all that beauty He placed on this earth just for us. Why, look over there at the woods. See the light dancing on the leaves, and the squirrels scurrying around, and the birds, listen to them sing to their Maker! The world all around us is happy and beautiful. It's full of God's beautiful gifts to us - all of us, saint and sinner alike. He loves us all, and he gives all these gifts for our senses to enjoy and take in so we will realize just how very much He loves us. Why, some days my heart just near bursts when I see all this beauty and know it's all saying, "I love you. - I LOVE **YOU!**"

What a God we serve!

Whew, just a second, let me wipe these tears out of my eyes.

Do you remember the very first time that person you loved so deeply and longingly said, "I love you"? The joy that just explodes inside you and turns your world into sunshine and roses everywhere you look? That's how I feel when I look - really look - at all this wondrous beauty He gives us just to say, "I love you". Oh my, if there was nothing else but His glorious sunset exclamation marks at the end of our day, before the dark of night sweeps across our skies, that alone should set our hearts to singing and praising our most gracious Lord! He washes the sky and clouds with breathtaking colors of the rainbow, just to say, "Good night, I love you." How can we ever thank Him enough for all He, our Lord, has done and does for us every day? Talk about miracles! Look around you, they're everywhere to be found, every day!

Yet we say, "I've never seen a miracle. If only I could see a real miracle of God." Brothers, sisters, sinner, and saint, look around you! God has placed before you the most wonderful miracles every day.

Truly, GREAT is our GOD, and GREATLY to be PRAISED!!!

SONNY'S FIRST CRY
[Still Born]
~ 2 ~

Ah, but now let me tell you about another miracle our precious Lord performed in the lives of our miracle family. Let's see, I guess the next miracle is one many of us have come to take for granted every day: the birth of a baby boy. But let me back up and start at the beginning of this segment in their lives.

Maurice and Mary Helen had been married four years when their love conceived their first child. I didn't hear of any problems or difficulties occurring during this blessed pregnancy, and as the birth of their child grew near, they became more anxious to find out if it was a boy or girl, and discussed names to be given to this precious gift from God; a gift of their love. As the awaited date came and labor started, it would be that bitter sweetness of pain and birth which would bring their child into this world, to bathe in their love. It was time; they would soon hold their precious newborn baby in their arms. With anticipation, they headed to the hospital and its arrival.

But, something was wrong. The doctor finally told them their baby was dead, it would be stillborn. How could that be? She had done everything the doctor had told her to do; the baby was pronounced well and healthy at her last check-up. What had happened to her baby? It was now too late for a normal birth, or even for a caesarean birth, as the baby was wedged too deep in the birth canal. Mary Helen's pelvis did not widen to allow for the birth of the child, so she would have to be deeply sedated and the baby forcibly pulled out of her body. Although physical damage could be done to the infant, they would be as careful as they possibly could and try not to do any more harm than necessary. Besides, the baby was already dead. Right now their main concern had to be Mary Helen.

Paperwork concerning the baby's stillbirth had to be completed for the hospital records, giving them authority to release the infant to the funeral home.

Maurice refused to leave the surgery area where his wife was fighting for her life, so Cora, Maurice's mother, went to the office to give the hospital all the information they needed. When asked what the baby was to be named, Cora thought for a minute or two and then decided not to use the name Maurice and Mary Helen had chosen. She would give the dead baby, their first- born son, his father's name; maybe they could have another baby someday and give it their chosen name. She named the baby Maurice Leroy Marquart, Maurice, after his father, and Leroy, after Mary Helen's father, Earl Leroy Pierce. Maurice Senior's name was Maurice Ervin Marquart.

Dave, Maurice's father, had been told the baby was dead and had been "shelved" for the morticians arrival, and doctors were doing all they knew to do to save Mary Helen's life; her body was badly damaged during the removal of the baby.

The death of the child hung heavy over the whole hospital that day; it was a small community, and everyone was either

Great is Our God... and Greatly to Be Praised!

family, a friend, or a neighbor. The father was Dave's boy, the one who had come back from the dead. Now this! Could this family survive another blow like this? What if Mary Helen died - Would Maurice survive the death of both his child and his wife? Would their faith hold up under all this? Would God step in and keep Mary Helen? Would they find peace in their faith for the funeral that lay ahead of them? Would it be a double funeral: mother and child? The questions swirled in the minds and hearts of all that day. "Oh God, how can one family bear so much pain and suffering," were the thoughts and worries in the minds of all those surrounding them on this fateful day.

Meanwhile, as the struggle between life and death continued in the delivery room, Dave quietly found a wooden bench across the hall, and kneeling beside it, began to pray quietly. It didn't matter to Dave what people might think of him kneeling in the hall of that hospital, or for that matter, whether people were around or not. He was talking with God, and that's all that mattered at a time like this; no one could help them. No one could save his daughter-in-law. No one could give them the strength of heart and soul to survive the events of this day - no one but God.

As he was kneeling there praying, he heard a man say, "Dave, Dave, what's the matter? Why are you praying?" Dave opened his eyes and turned to look up at the man standing beside him, a man who knew his name, but one he had no recollection of ever seeing before, he did not know this man.

Again, the man said, "Dave, what's the matter, why are you praying? Get up, tell me what's wrong." So Dave rose to his feet and began telling the man, "My grandchild is dead, it was a boy, and my daughter-in-law is in there [pointing to the door] fighting for her life. The doctors don't think she is going to live, her chances are so slim."

In the soft, calm voice of the stranger, Dave heard, "Dave, where have they put the baby?"

Dave, now bewildered by the sorrow gripping his heart and the stranger's question, pointed to a door down the hall. "They've put his body down there, in the room down there."

Softly the man said, "Dave, take me down to the room where they have put him, show me where they have laid your grandson."

So, Dave and the stranger walked down the hall to the door. Dave opened the door and went over to a little shelf on the wall where his grandson laid, his face torn and one eye seriously damaged by the forceps used to free his body from his mother's womb. As Dave stood looking at the body of his grandson, almost forgetting the stranger who stood at his side, the stranger quietly stepped around Dave, and without a word spoken, placed the fingers of his right hand upon the forehead of the dead baby.

The baby began to cry!!!

Can you imagine the shock that swept through Dave's body, the shock, and the joy of his beloved grandson coming to life! Hardly believing his own eyes, Dave turned to thank the stranger, but there was no kind stranger there!!! He rushed out into the hall, but there was no glorious stranger walking down the halls or going out the door. There was no one who had seen him or knew which way he had gone. Th is wonderful, life-giving stranger had just vanished, never to be seen again, as far as I know.

Now, I'm not saying who the stranger was for sure, but I know what I felt and believed in my heart when I heard about this miracle, what Maurice and Mary Helen believed, and their family. Just as three men came walking across the land and Abraham ran out and called "Lord", one who announced there would be a son born[30]; one came walking into that hospital on Oct. 19, 1940, and touched a little baby boy on the forehead and gave him life.

GREAT is our GOD, and GREATLY to be PRAISED!!!

I am fully persuaded there is not one promise, one gift, or one visitation of God, or angels, in the bible that we cannot have in our day and time. I am also fully persuaded our Lord is the same today as He was for Abraham, Moses, Paul[31] and everyone else who had personal experiences with our Lord. We can have anything the Word shows us was experienced by one of His children or followers; it's all up to us. Just how important is it to experience the deep things of God, to walk in His presence and will? I truly believe with all my heart there is only one thing hindering us: US! *"For there is no respect of persons with God."* Romans 2:10-11[32]

Grab hold of the horns of the altar, wrestle with the powers that assail you, and refuse to let go until you have talked one-on-one with the Lord, until YOU know the heart and mind of God. Until you also hear those words spoken to Daniel, "Oh, [insert your name], a (wo)man greatly beloved. From the first day you set your heart to understand, your words were heard"[33] Herein is another possible key, "set your heart to understand." Have we really "set our hearts" to understanding God's word, will, purpose, and plan for our lives?

How much do we desire, need, down deep in our souls to understand, to be one with our Lord and Savior? Does this "need" drive us to our knees every opportunity we get to call out to God? Does it leave us weeping in our beds at night deeply desiring that walk in our Lord?

I'm reminded of some words of a chorus . . ."

♪
Oh to be His hand extended,
Reaching out to the oppressed.
Let me touch Him, let me touch Jesus,
So that others may know and be blessed
♪[34]

Is this the cry of your heart, from the very depth of your soul? Let me touch Jesus! Let me touch Jesus!!! Does every cell within your being cry out in desperation, "Let me touch Jesus!"

He's there, waiting, just for YOU.

Oh, what a God, what a God we serve! He stands waiting patiently, longingly for us to love Him the way He loves us. How is it we daily put everything before Him. Daily we remind Him He is not first in our heart and life, but second, third, fiftieth. How have we become so hardened by this world and our wants and desires that we can daily grieve our Lord's heart by saying, "Not now, later Lord; one day, Lord, I'll put you first in my life." Our days come and go; we're twelve, then twenty-nine, then fifty, and still He stands waiting, knocking at our heart's door.[35]

Oh my Lord and my God, forgive me. Oh Lord, help me to learn to put you first in my life every day and in every situation, My Lord, Jehovah God, I desire you to be first in my heart, soul, and mind, in every thought and step I take. Please God, by your precious Holy Spirit, teach me how to put you first, now and for always in every situation! Teach me to love you, as You love me."

Oh I'm sorry, forgive me. I need to get back to our story; it's just that He loves us so much! And all He wants back is for us to love Him.

Of course, the doctor, being an unbeliever at the time, held no hope for this baby boy to be a normal child, it just couldn't happen. He had been dead, without oxygen to his brain for far too long. This baby would be a vegetable - brain dead - he wouldn't survive long. A human being just cannot go without oxygen for that length of time, it's just impossible.

When mother and baby were well enough, Maurice and Mary Helen took their beautiful baby boy home to love him and to raise him to be the best he could be, for as long as he lived. He was a gift from God, brought back from the grave, and God's gifts always brought blessings. Gifts of heartache and pain always brought growth and blessings beyond human wisdom and understanding; they would wait on the Lord and cherish the precious gift His will had bestowed on them.

I know what you may be thinking, how can a new baby whose face was physically torn and damaged, a baby who was proclaimed to be mentally deficient, a vegetable, be considered a gift of God. Not to mention all the pain and damage Mary Helen's body suffered through his birth; how can any of this be a gift of God?

First of all, a thought just flashed through my mind, all the pain and suffering of our Lord as he labored through cruelty, scourging, and death, to birth our access to the throne of God; providing the way for us to become true sons and daughters of God through the suffering of Christ. The word of God says, "Greater love hath no man than this, that a man lay down his life for his friends." John 15:13[36]

It is my belief a true mother's heart is like unto our Lord's, willing to suffer and lay down her life if necessary to birth that new creation of God into this world. Then, after birth, to cherish, protect, and guide that child to be all he or she can be. This sometimes takes the love of discipline, or the knowledge that a little sorrow, suffering, or pain now can help us grow and develop into a better, nicer person in the future; a person who has gained in understanding and skill to become our best. Isn't that just like our Lord, chastening those whom He loves so they may grow and become perfect, mature, in Him.[37]

Charles G. Finney[38] said, "When it becomes real to us that we owe everything to God, our health, gifts, all our comforts, then we can bear many dark and trying things." You may remember how Cecil[39] taught his little daughter the meaning of gospel faith. She came to him, one day, with her hands full of little beads, greatly delighted, to show them. He said to her calmly, "You had better throw them all into the fire." She was almost confounded; but, when she saw he was in earnest, she trustfully obeyed, and cast them in. After a few days, he brought home for her a casket of jewels. "There," said he, "my daughter, you had faith in me the other day, and threw your beads into the fire. That was faith. Now I can give you things much more precious. Are not these far better?" So you should always believe in God. He has jewels for those who will believe. Judgments and chastisements are the rebukes of God, for all these, too, are means of grace, and are blessed of

God for the spiritual good of his children. Their only design as they come from our Father's hand is that they may work out good to his saints. He does not afflict willingly, nor grieve the children of men from caprice (whim, impulse), or from any pleasure in their pain, but only and wholly for their profit, that they may the more deeply "partake of his holiness."

"Under this broad principle, we know that all the losses and crosses which befall the saints, all their burdens of care and responsibility, and all their infirmities, shall be overruled for their good. All these things will conspire to teach the saints more of God and more of themselves."[40]

That last part pretty much explains why we as God's children suffer and go through hard times. Let me cut it down to the core of his message. "He, God, does not afflict willingly, from caprice (whim, impulse), or from any pleasure in their pain, but only and wholly <u>for their profit, that they may</u> the more deeply "<u>partake of his holiness</u>." . . . <u>All the losses . . . crosses</u> which befall the saints, . . . <u>all burdens . . . all</u> their <u>infirmities</u>, shall be overruled for their good. <u>All these things will conspire to teach the saints more of God and more of themselves.</u>" Short and simple, he allows those things to happen for our own good. When we truly realize that fact, it would be wise of us to seek out the truth or lesson we need to learn at our earliest opportunity. The sooner we learn our lesson, the quicker we can graduate from that class of hard knocks. As God's child, we must always remember: "And we know that all things work together for good to them that love God, to them who are the called according to his purpose." Romans 8:2[41]

Come on, say it with me, "<u>ALL</u> THINGS work together for good." Again, out loud, "<u>ALL</u> THINGS WORK TOGETHER FOR GOOD, all things."

This is where I borrow a cliché about the word "no". What don't you understand about the word **"all"**? Now, just in case you think I'm pointing my finger at you when I say that, remember there are three fingers pointing back at me. I must continually keep this truth in the forefront of my mind. ALL things are for my good. It is my job sometimes to seek out that good. Is it a blessing I am experiencing, a lesson to be learned, or a chastisement for a wrong I've committed? When speaking to some Jews who believed in Him, Jesus said, "If ye continue in my word, then are ye my disciples indeed; And ye shall know the truth, and the truth shall make you free." John 8:31-32[42]

Continue in His word, He will reveal the truth to a sincere, seeking heart.

A DEVASTATING DILEMMA
[Mary Helen's]
~ 3 ~

Mary Helen's difficulties with birthing her first-born son appeared to start a chain reaction of physical problems. For some reason, it was believed there was a connection to the birth of their son and an episode that occurred about four or five months later.

It was a fairly normal day, as normal as it could be for someone who had undergone so much physical damage. Mary Helen was trying to busy herself doing all the normal duties of a new mother and wife of four years, when she was asked by her brother "Junior", Earl Leroy Pierce Jr., if she would like to go for a little ride. It all sounded so good to her, riding around in the crisp cool air after being cooped up either in the hospital or at home most of the time since the birth of their son. Junior was such a good brother, thinking of things like rides in the countryside. Somehow, a ride in the country always seemed to make her feel better as she looked at all the work of our Lord's creation. She just seemed to become renewed in her strength, as she thought on the love of God to give us all these wonderful things to look on. There were rolling hills with cattle grazing on the hill sides; horses frolicking in the cool sunshine; pigs rooting through the snow sprinkled ground in the mash put out for them that morning; and watching the cloudy mist of breath of the animals standing at the fence line as they slowly rode by. She loved it all. Her heavenly Father gave this all for her to enjoy.

I really can't recall if they had stopped for a little walk on one of the two business streets of the town or if they were still riding in the car, but I seem to recall something about grabbing and hanging on to a light pole when her day was once again turned upside down. Mary Helen was suddenly struck with excruciating pain in her lower abdomen, unbearable pain that just kept mounting in severity. She was again rushed to the closest hospital, where it was determined she was having a serious appendix attack and would need immediate surgery.

Once again, time crawled as Maurice rushed to be by the side of his wife, and once again, he paced the halls of the hospital surgery department; when would the doctor be done and come out? How was his precious wife and soul mate, would she be all right? It seemed like an eternity to him.

He recalled how good life had been for them and how they were so happy before they were married and during the first four years of marriage. But since then, starting with the birth of their son, his beautiful wife had suffered so much, and now this. They were only twenty-three and had already gone through his wreck and death, the birth of their stillborn son with the diagnosis of serious brain damage, and now this. What could be wrong?

Great is Our God... and Greatly to Be Praised!

Maurice turned, circling the end of the hall, to walk back toward the surgery doors when the doctor walked out into the hall and up to him.

The doctor's face was sad, his gaze cast down to the floor, as he said, "Maurice, Mary Helen is pregnant, she's going to have another baby. When she comes out from under the sedation, someone is going to have to tell her. I'm going to have to tell her she is going to have another baby. Maurice, I don't know if our Mary can survive the birth of another child."

NO, NO, it can't be! Every bone in his body wanted to scream out into the dead air engulfing him, but he stood there in silence, dead silence, unable to speak. How could this be? How could this be happening to them, to his dear, sweet Mary? What's going to happen to her! The silence could have been cut with a knife as they stood there, the doctor's hand on his back trying to console him as best he could, but his heart was breaking, too.

After some time passed, he didn't know how long, Maurice said, "I'll tell her, I need to be the one to tell her." The doctor, a long-time friend, said, "Maurice, we didn't think we were going to be able to save her during the birth of your son. Now this appendix attack and surgery, and another birth in seven or eight months, I just don't see how her body can go through all that and survive. I'm afraid we are going to lose our Mary."

I truthfully cannot remember if what I am about to tell you happened at this time, during the appendix surgery, or later during the caesarean birth of their baby four or five months later (not seven or eight months as it should have been). But during one of these times, it was discovered that due to the traumatic birth of their son, Maurice L., 'Sonny', almost all of Mary Helen's organs had either sagged extensively or were torn away from their normal support systems. How she must have been suffering. Suffering without complaint and trying to be and do everything a wife and mother is supposed to do. Th ank God for mothers! Her mother, Mary, was doing all she could to help her daughter. When God made "mothers" He poured all His love into their hearts, His love for sons and daughters birthed by the suffering of His Son. At least some mothers are like that, and her mother was one of those precious loving mothers.

Due to the inability of her organs and body to function properly or receive proper nourishment, the doctor would have to stitch each organ back in place to prevent them from further damage and shutting down. Her body was like a battlefield, torn, and damaged.

So he began. It was never said if the doctor ever explained why he did what he did, but he began stitching one organ after the other back in place, oriented as it should be, painstakingly, meticulously stitch after stitch after stitch; a long tedious job. For some reason he was determined to stitch every organ in place without ever breaking the surgical thread, maybe he felt a continuous stitch would give more strength and stability. Maybe he was reaching for anything that could give Mary the slightest chance to survive! Could he stitch life back into this tiny little body? Could he make it hold until her body could begin to heal and mend itself? After meticulously stitching everything carefully back in the place it was meant to be, the doctor tied off the thread to the beginning thread, forming one continuous circle. The doctor then closed her up and hoped for Mary Helen to survive the ordeal that lay ahead of her.

You see, Maurice and Mary Helen meant a lot to the doctor. They were his first patients, the first ones to trust him after he came back from the war an alcoholic. No one in town would even walk through his office doors. They weren't going to trust their lives or the lives of their children to a drunk. But Maurice and Mary Helen changed all that.

One day, when life seemed normal and good, before Maurice's death, Maurice and Mary Helen walked into his empty office and asked to speak to the doctor. The nurse/receptionist, the doctor's wife, told them he'd be right out and quickly went to get the doctor. When he came out and asked what he could do for them, Maurice said, "We have decided to have you for our doctor. But, if you ever treat one of us in a drunken state, or show up in the office or hospital to treat one of us in a drunken state, that will be the last time you ever treat anyone in our family. Understood?"

The doctor was so grateful for the opportunity to prove himself to them and to the community, he readily agreed to Maurice's terms.

He had been a good doctor, but the war just, well he just couldn't let go of all he had seen and all the death and dying replaying in his mind. So many boys were maimed or dead. Maybe he would be given the chance to do what he went into medicine to do: cure, heal, and save lives.

As he proved his dependability to Maurice and Mary Helen, with the town watching, waiting for him to fail, he began to prove himself to the community. Slowly other patients began to trickle in, skeptical and uneasy at first, but he would be patient and very grateful for this chance to become respectable and trusted again. The doctor and his wife always said they owed his career, their livelihood, and their eventual standing in the community to Maurice and Mary Helen and their willingness to take a chance with him. The doctor felt he owed them his best at all times; besides, they had become friends. He never, ever wanted to let them down. When times were hard and they could not pay their whole bill, it didn't matter, it was because of them he had any medical practice at all. Besides, they would pay it, all of it, as they could. He never realized how big that bill would become, or how much care they would need.

You know, one of the thoughts that crossed my mind as I was telling you about the doctor, I wonder how many other doctors would have fought so hard for this little family of four. How many would have waited so long for their bills to be paid. It just seems to me their willingness to give him a chance paid off abundantly. Isn't that just like our God, pairing off a young married couple with a drunken doctor, knowing each would be just what was needed in the future? It was a God thing, saving the lives of both parties; one socially, the other physically. Each needed the other.

Hey, do a favor for me, Okay?

Keep this connection in mind as you hear more of their story. Would all of these miracles have taken place if they had not joined in willing obedience to God's plan; if Maurice and Mary Helen had never given the doctor a chance? Would the other doctors have fought so hard, given so tirelessly of their time and efforts, even when bills couldn't be paid? One had a present need to be given a chance; in the future, the other would have a desperate need for an exceptional doctor. Sometimes, when shuffling through the rejects of this world, one finds a gem, one of God's diamonds in the rough.

"Oh Lord, help me to find your diamonds - struggling, encased by all the filth this world has heaped upon them - give me spiritual eyes to see them, and long, loving hands to reach out, strength of spirit and will to pull them from the miry clay and give them a chance to shine again. Precious, Holy Father, let not one of your diamonds be lost! Send loving hands to lift them into your light and care, into your perfect plan for their lives. Let them shine, let them glow, reflecting the light of Your love."

AGAINST ALL ODDS
[ConnieJean's Birth]
~ 4 ~

Everyone watched, helped, and encouraged Maurice and Mary Helen as they watched the doctor's sad predictions appear to come true. This baby was sapping the very life out of her. Mary Helen's body was so damaged, so weak, and there was more. A new problem emerged. There was the constant threat this baby might miscarry since the damage to her uterus was so extensive. Once the new life in Mary Helen began to move and stretch its little arms and legs, they found her damage from the birth of their son and the proceeding surgeries had left her abdomen very weak and thin, with almost no muscle tone.

As the little embryo within her began to develop and buds became little hands and feet, and the merging life began to shift and turn, they could actually see the form of its little fingers, toes, and elbows, as it pressed against the walls of her uterus and abdomen. The doctor repeatedly told Mary Helen he would have to take this child. If he didn't, she would not live through the baby's birth; they would both die. But she was not going to give up her baby, her child, without a fight. She would do whatever she had to do, but she would not allow her child to be taken until it could survive.

Days went by, then a month, then three. Now Mary Helen was bedridden and most of the time her mother, Mary, sat at her side. Each time the baby inside her would move or stretch, Mary would gently lay her hand upon that finger, elbow, knee, or foot, and gently, oh so gently, press it back down into her body, she was doing her best to become the muscles Mary Helen no longer had to constrain this growing child.

Finally, the day came when the doctor did something he had never done to Maurice or Mary Helen before. He lied. Mary Helen's abdomen and uterus had become so thin from the birth of their first-born thirteen months earlier and the poking and prodding of this new life, that he feared it would punch right through her body and both would die. He had to save at least one of them, and that had to be Mary Helen. She still had a chance to survive.

He lied to save her life. He told Mary Helen the baby was now far enough along to survive, and they needed to take it right away, but in his heart he felt there was no chance for this little struggling child to live; it was too early, too fragile. But he assured Mary Helen the baby could survive, and he would do everything in his power to see that it did. So she consented, and the baby was taken caesarean on December 10, 1941, one year and fifty-two days after the birth and resurrection of their first child, Sonny.

They named it ConnieJean. I say 'it' because this baby didn't look like a baby at all. It was too early, it wasn't finished developing. ConnieJean had no hair, no eyebrows, no eyelashes; she had no fingernails or toenails, and her flesh was so extremely sensitive she could not even be held. This new little bundle of joy was the height of a small catsup bottle, looked like a skinned rabbit in a butcher store, and couldn't be touched. The doctor fought with all he had in him to keep this baby breathing just another minute, another hour, another day. I heard tell he stayed around the clock many days, especially in the beginning, to be with Mary Helen and ConnieJean to make sure they would make it through another night.

I do not know how much time passed before the doctor let Mary Helen and ConnieJean go home from the hospital, back to her family and friends. But ConnieJean still could not be held. She would have to lie on a little pillow and be carried around on that pillow, so as not to touch her highly sensitive skin any more than absolutely necessary. Mary Helen said she was so tiny they could make her pillow bed in a shoebox; I wonder if they did. They said she screamed in pain every time she was even lightly touched by human hands.

Maybe she just didn't like this new world she was forced into. What do you think?

Can you just imagine what it would be like, to go home to a thirteen month old and a screaming "it" in the physical condition Mary Helen was in at that time? And there was not one beautiful, normal, baby in the batch; not one to be shown off with proud buttons popping. The fruit of their love appeared to produce only pain, heartache, and damaged fruit. But they would never have to worry about giving birth to "less than normal" children again. The doctor made sure Mary Helen could not become pregnant again; she would never sacrifice her health or her life to bring another little one into this world.

Oh, how her mother and father's heart must have grieved for their young, beautiful daughter. Mary Helen had been so outstandingly beautiful and so outgoing and healthy, energetic and fun loving; now she was racked with various problems from the trauma her body had endured. Life was hard, and there was little or no money to pay the volcanic bills that mounted higher and higher threatening to bury them under its fallout. Determined, they did everything they could, as soon as they could; and they just kept plodding along believing in God and trusting Him.

Why? Why did God allow all these things to happen to them? Why did they have to suffer and struggle so much?

Oh my friend, we must remember, "ALL things work together for good ..."

How could all that suffering, and two less-than-normal babies, have been seen as something good?

Wait a minute, hold on; I know you can't see it now and its upsetting to our human way of thinking, but do you remember what the word says in Isaiah 55:8-9[43] "For my thoughts are not your thoughts, neither are your ways my ways, saith the LORD. For as the heavens are higher than the earth, so are my ways higher than your ways, and my thoughts than your thoughts"?

We have to **know** that our **Father knows best**! You and I cannot look out into the future and know how every circumstance is going to affect our future, or anyone else's. How do we dare question God's ways, isn't that the same as saying we think we know more than God about the situation? We have to trust Him. Paul said, "...when I am weak, then am I strong" 2 Corinthians 12:8-10[44] Now, how can we be both weak and strong? When we are weak in our flesh, we become strong in our spirit, we become more and more dependent on God when we get to that place where we are at the end of our rope and just don't know what to do, or which way to turn. Our Lord says, ". . . My grace is sufficient for thee: for my strength is made perfect in weakness. . ."[45] Here, he is saying <u>His strength</u> is made perfect, it's complete (able to complete, finish, bring to an end; add what is missing) in our weakness, so His power may rest upon us. He, our Lord, has the power to complete, bring to an end, or to add what is missing in our lives to accomplish whatever is needed in our lives and in the lives of those we are meant to touch by our experiences; our weaknesses. We are not an island living only unto ourselves, but each of us is like the center of a vast chain reaction; my life affects you and your life affects another as it ripples through your family, friends, church, neighborhood – anyone and everyone you meet. Only God can line up the right people and cause the right ripple to pass from one to another so that all are affected for good, but we must be submissive to His will and weak to our fleshly thoughts and desires. For some it may take illness, a disability, a loss, or a sorrow to bring our flesh into a place of weakness, depending not on self but surrendering to our Lord's will and guidance. When we have the reins in our hands and keep tugging on them, and trying to turn what seems to us like run-away events in our lives, we force our wills and make things go the way we think they should. Just like Balaam,[46] we are fighting against the very thing that will bring us into perfection, completion, in our Lord. Let go of the reins! Trust Him! By His power become complete, perfect, through your weakness - just let go.

Paul said he would glory in his infirmities[47] Why? Because he knew there is no vacuum. We are vessels that must be full; the flesh must decrease that the spirit may increase. In the words of John the Baptist "He must increase (grow, become greater), but I must decrease (become less, inferior)." John 3:30[48]

Oh, wow, I really got into that, didn't I?

Speaking from personal experience, it is my belief the two, no three, hardest things to do are: <u>lean not unto thine own understanding, let go of the reins</u>, and <u>become weak</u> for Christ's sake. That the power of Christ may rest upon me.

BUT, if we sincerely want, or need, miracles to be manifested in our lives and ministries, that is exactly what we must do!

I'm sure, just like the rest of us, there must have been times they became discouraged and questioned their lives and decisions they had made, and wondered where it all went wrong. Had they somehow brought this all on themselves?

Well, let me tell you one more thing before we take a little break here. I don't know about you, but I am tiring out a bit. You've been listening to me for quite a while now. Are your ears beginning to tune out and your brain shutting down yet?

No?!

Okay, if you really want to.

What was I saying?

Oh, right!

Mary Helen and the little ones were both home, and everyone was doing their best to do their best. Talk about a household of sickies! Maurice was still suffering from the queen of windshields screeching, "Off with his head!" Mary Helen still had complications from her last ordeal. Sonny's damaged eye wandered every which way when he tried to focus, and ConnieJean, well, everyone tried to leave her alone and hoped she'd sleep a good long time before the 'screaming banshee' woke up the whole neighborhood. When it really got bad and nothing would quiet her down, it was off for a drive through the countryside until their little sleeping beauty (if you can imagine a skinned rabbit as being beautiful) munched on sandman's apple and nodded off again. It was a brave thing to go back home and turn off that key, brave indeed!

I guess everything was humming along pretty normal, at least for this household.

Sometime, either during this pregnancy or after Mary Helen and ConnieJean went home, God sent them a message, a message of hope. That's the way the doctor saw it, anyway. My understanding is that the doctor wasn't really a believer in God, at least not before his experiences with M&M (Maurice and Mary Helen).

Do you remember me telling you how the doctor sewed all of Mary Helen's organs back in place with one continuous surgical thread?

You know, come to think of it, I believe it was following the birth of ConnieJean. You see, Mary Helen had developed deep, seeping cysts in her abdomen, five of them. I can't remember if anything was said as to what exactly was suspected to have caused these cysts, but Mary Helen would have to go in to the doctor's office and have the cysts drained from time to time. It was on one of those office visits that the doctor said, "Oh, I see one of the threads has worked its way up to the surface. I'd better take it out."

The doctor took his surgical tweezers, and began to pull out the piece of thread he had spotted. After it began to come out, he noted it was two threads side by side. He pulled, and pulled, and pulled a little more. "Hmm," he said, "this is a little longer than I thought." He continued to pull on the thread slowly and gently, until finally it came to an end, one complete circle with one knot holding both the ends together!

He stood looking at this circle he was holding in his hands, staring at it. Then he said, "There must be a God."

He later cleaned, mounted, and framed the circle of love, and hung it on his office wall to remind him of God's part in this business called medicine. To him, only God could have pulled off this miracle. It was not the doing of any physician, nor did it have anything to do with the consistency of the thread. He checked. There was a God, there had to be. It was God, not him, that was keeping this family alive time after time, against all odds!

Who would have thought, a piece of thread would convince this doctor of the existence of God, when a severed head and resurrection didn't; when a stillborn baby's cry could not; when Mary Helen's battles, which brought her to death's door repeatedly, did not; and the fact that ConnieJean was a living force to be reckoned with. Not one of them should have been alive by human standards and thinking.

A simple piece of thread!

Would you have thought a simple piece of thread would have stopped anyone dead in their tracks and turned a non-believer into a believer?

I sure wouldn't!

Why do you suppose Mary Helen's organs were allowed to become so damaged they had to be sewn back in place? Why was she allowed to develop complications and seeping cysts? I can't say for sure, my thoughts are not God's thoughts, but one thing I know, there was a doctor who did not believe in God - who **now** believed.

"Trust in the LORD with all thine heart; and lean not unto thine own understanding." Proverbs 3:5[49]

Was he worth it?

"I say unto you, that likewise joy shall be in heaven over one sinner that repenteth, more than over ninety and nine just persons, which need no repentance." Luke 15:7[50]

Would you like to know what I think? I think it was also a symbol of the circle of love from God to Maurice and Mary Helen and from them back to God again, knotted and tied securely. Nothing could dissolve that circle of love unless they personally untied the knot, a sign from God to tell them He was there, always; He was in control, and everything would be all right.

Could this be another clue as to why this family had so many unexplained, humanly impossible events happening in their lives (those things we call miracles). They had taken their end of the line between them and God, handed it up to God saying in their hearts, "Here God, it's all up to you." God had tied it securely by His love so that no man could break or dissolve their circle of love saying " . . . fear not . . . the Lord thy God . . . doth go with thee . . . will not fail thee . . . nor forsake thee"[51] "And I will make an everlasting covenant with them, that I will not turn away from them, to do them good; but I will put my fear in their hearts, that they shall not depart from me."[52]

The word says, "For I am persuaded, that neither death, nor life, nor angels, nor principalities, nor powers, nor things present, nor things to come, Nor height, nor depth, nor any other creature, shall be able to separate us from the love of God, which is in Christ Jesus our Lord." Romans 8:38-39[53] "But when Jesus heard it, he answered him, saying, Fear not: believe only, and she shall be made whole." Luke 8:50[54]

Were they fully persuaded nothing could separate them from the love of God, which is in Christ Jesus our Lord? Did they know nothing, no matter what came their way, could pull them out of God's loving hands; they would always be held in the love of God?

We all need to grow to that place in our relationship with our Lord, when we know that we know His love will never leave us nor forsake us. We will always be covered by His love, encircled, enveloped in His precious ever-present love and care. Whether in times of hardship and sorrow, or in times of joy and gladness, He is always there holding us in the center of His hand. We see and only understand what is happening in our world during the present, we cannot see as our Lord sees into the far out-reaching future.

We cannot know all the good that will come from our times of hardship; the fruit it will produce for ourselves or for others. It is only for us to know our Lord loves us and has only the best for us in His plan for our lives. Are we being tested so we can be made stronger? Will our tests and trials lead us to a new and better understanding of God and His word in our lives? Is there fruit of souls which God desires to bring into His fold through us; by the way we travel through our hard times and influence others? Do you remember the story of Lazarus in the bible? What did Jesus say about Lazarus' sickness? "When Jesus heard that, he said, "This sickness is not unto death, but for the glory of God, that the Son of God might be glorified thereby."" John 1:4[55]

We don't know the answers to these questions until sometime long after the hardship has passed, if then. But our love and trust of our Lord must be so embedded, so ingrained, in our heart, soul, and mind, that nothing sways us from our knowledge of the truth: He has us in His hands and we are exactly where we need to be if we want to be in the center of His will. Keep your eyes upon our Lord and Savior, not on the circumstances in this world.

Oh that God's ultimate plan would be that our lives might bring glory to him and glorify his son, Jesus! As I write this testimony of their lives, I wonder, could it all have been for *you*? Did they go through all those events in their lives so that you might hear and believe? Is it possible our heavenly Father will be glorified by their suffering and glorious miracles through your growth and deeper walk with Him? That you might hear and believe, truly believe all things are possible to them that believe, come what may, you too, can reach out to Him and be healed!

"Oh Lord, Jehovah, let it be so.

'KABOOSKI' & 'KANEKA'
[Sonny & ConnieJean]
~ 5 ~

As the days passed by, Sonny grew and seemed normal enough. In fact, he became a happy little boy who Earl, Mary Helen's father, would call his little "Chunny Man" and who Maurice called his little 'Kabooski' (I suspect Sonny followed his daddy everywhere). What a joy he was to them; he was a ray of sunshine! Just imagine how it would feel each time they looked into the chubby little face of that happy baby boy knowing he had been brought back from death, how it must have felt when they watched him and saw no signs of mental deprivation. He seemed, to them, to be okay for a little boy his age. How their hearts must have turned to praise and worship to God every time they looked on this precious gift from God. Sonny, even at a very early age, seemed to have developed such a care and love for his little baby sister, even though he could not touch or play with her. He seemed so drawn to her. I was told he just liked to be near her, play near where she was sleeping. It seems from the time he was able to talk, his little "sissy" wouldn't be ignored or left out. If she couldn't have it, whatever 'it' was, then he didn't want it either. He'd say, "And one for sissy?" when offered a treat or toy. He was sissy's little guardian angel and was always looking out for her, protecting her as best he could.

But ConnieJean, Mary Helen's 'Jeannie', was a very sick little girl. As time passed, and she became older, she remained sickly; always fragile, always frail.

At the age of two, ConnieJean received a doll for Christmas; a thirty-six inch doll that stood at least a head taller than she did. It was quite comical watching her try to carry her 'Jeannie' from one place to another. I was told at the age of two, ConnieJean finally had enough hair to wrap in a pin-curl to make her pretty. At three she only weighed nineteen pounds and stood about the height of three or four building foundation blocks (height, not length); the bodice of her little homemade dress, sewn with great love and care, was only 1½ - 2" long.

ConnieJean, Maurice's little 'KaNeka' (pronounced Ka-Knee-ka), was unable to run and play like other three-year-old toddlers; she had developed a mysterious health problem which the doctor felt sure was due to her premature birth. It seemed in those days, everything, no matter what it was, somehow became labeled: "due to her premature birth." If allowed to get up and move around much at all, she would lose any weight she had been able to accumulate. She just could not maintain any weight. A cow was given to Maurice and Mary Helen by a very kind farmer to supply ConnieJean with some daily fresh cream (and milk for the family), in order to try and fatten her up, and build up her weight and stamina. Can you imagine that happening today, allowing a cow in the center of town!

Great is Our God... and Greatly to Be Praised!

Oh, how very different things were back in those days, when people really cared about their neighbor's needs and not so much about what 'just wouldn't be right, look right, or smell right,' like having a cow in town. I was told as long as she didn't get off the couch and ate everything they gave her, she wouldn't lose more weight and might even gain an ounce or two here and there. But when she got off the couch and played like a normal toddler for just an hour or two, the weight would begin to drop off. No one could figure it out. The only conclusion the doctor was able to come up with was that her digestive system had probably not completely developed by the time she was born.

But I know One who knew all along what was ailing their little girl. One who would keep her in the palm of His hand and protect her, keep her safe. We can always, ALWAYS, trust our Lord to know, and to do, the best for us.

Oh, how does that song go?

♪

> Turn your eyes upon Jesus,
> look full in His wonderful face,
> and the things of this earth
> will grow strangely dim,
> in the light of His glory and grace
>
> ♪56

"This is the cry of my heart every day, that my eyes be turned upon my loving Lord so that one day I will look full in His wonderful face!"

We will victoriously cross any ocean of sorrow, any wilderness of pain and defeat, and any night of testing, if we just keep our eyes upon Jesus!!! Like Peter, we can walk those seas of life[57] *if* we just keep our eyes and mind on our Lord! What a glorious key this is, a key to calm through the storms of life, a key when all about us seems to be falling apart at the seams, a key to living a victorious life in our Savior.

Did you notice, the winds and waves were boisterous and tossed and the disciples were troubled; just like we are when we are going through the storms of life. Did the storm around them vanish immediately when they saw Jesus? When they realized who Jesus was? When Peter mustered up enough faith to get out of the boat and go to Jesus *in* the storm? No. The storm still persisted all around them. As long as Peter kept his eyes on Jesus and not on the storm, his walk to Jesus was smooth sailing. It was when he got his eyes on the storm around him that he began to sink, and became afraid (worried, concerned). It's really important to remember we have three choices when it comes to weathering the storms of our lives:

1. We can stay in the boat of 'self' and fight the storms with our own knowledge and skills.
2. We can get out of the boat (self) and by faith get our eyes upon Him and walk where and how He provides the way. Remember, it's only easy going in the storm as long as we are focused on Jesus. When we focus on the storm, we will sink. Or,

3. We can get back into the boat '***with Jesus***' and give Him all authority and control of our boat (self) and He will calm the seas

Not only is there three choices, but I see here a progression; depending on self, turning to Jesus, being in the boat with Jesus, and then finally giving Him all authority and control of our lives. Just like Peter, we seem to turn to Jesus requesting His words of encouragement, "Come". But we, like Peter, take our eyes off of Jesus and begin again to look at the storm around us.

As we begin to sink down into the despair and hopelessness of our storm, we cry out to Him again, "Lord, save me!" and He once again comes to our rescue. As I see it, one of our biggest problems and hindrances in a victorious walk with our Lord is we keep cycling and re-cycling through stages one and two and never really get back into our boat, *with Christ totally in charge*. That is the only place where we will be able to find that 'perfect peace that passeth all understanding'. Philippians 4:7[58]

2 Corinthians 13:11[59] states we are to be of "one mind". What mind, whose mind? The mind of Christ; we are all to be one in the mind and will of our Lord.

Oh praise the Lord!!! All we have to do is focus. Keep our focus on our Messiah, our soon coming King, our Bridegroom. He will make "*. . . all things work together for good to them that love God, to them who are the called according to his purpose.*" Romans 8:28 [60]

Are you His child? Do you belong to Him? Then you are called according to His purpose. His word is just as true for you as it is for any Pastor or Evangelist. All things, not just the joyful things, not just the good feeling things, not just the words of praise, but ALL THINGS work together for good. In every situation and every circumstance, look for the good of our Lord. Is there a lesson you need to learn? Will His name and kingdom be glorified through you? Seek to see the good in all things. And when you just can't see it, then know, in faith, our Lord is working something out for your good.[61] <u>Faith believes </u>what you cannot see or feel at the moment <u>and knows</u>, in your heart and mind, <u>it's true</u>. As a child of the living God, if it says it in His word, we should know it in our heart to be true. If there had not been an accident and death, there could not have been a resurrection. If there had not been a stillborn baby boy, there would not have been a visit from a mysterious stranger sent by God (an angel unawares (Hebrews 13:2[62])). If there had not been a need for a laboriously stitched circle, there would not have been an unbelieving doctor who became a believer. There is a reason for *all* things in the life of a believer; and, all those things are for good! Rejoice in the good *and* hard times for God is working through you to do good![63]

 Oh, wow, look at the time! I really didn't realize how long I've been talking!

 Do you need to go?

 If not, let's go in the house and I'll fix us a bite to eat. Do you want more coffee or would you rather have a softdrink or raspberry ice tea?

 Let me see what I have in the house to make a sandwich. Would you like some homemade chicken and vegetable soup to go with your sandwich and raspberry iced tea? Hmm, guess I'm hungrier than I thought.

I'm such a terrible hostess to let you go this long without offering you anything but coffee! Would you rather eat inside or out on the patio?

Okay, inside it is.

The soup is warming, and these sandwiches are almost ready. Would you mind getting the tea out of the refrigerator? It's there on the middle shelf behind the two-percent milk.

Sure, I believe I'll have some tea, too.

Okay, if you really want to. The soup bowls and sandwich plates are in that cabinet over by the patio doors, behind the table. Glasses are in the cupboard on the right side of the sink, the tall ones on the top shelf. Oh, you know what; I believe there are some corn chips over there on the bread table if you'd like some with your soup and sandwich.

Oh, I just remembered, there are two pieces of the berry pie I made yesterday. We really liked it. We can finish it off, if you'd like some dessert.

Well, let's see, there are elderberries (with the seeds milled out), blueberries, and raspberries in it, about twice as much as you'll normally find in a pie. When I eat pie, I want it filled with the fruit, not a lot of that gooey filling!

Why don't you sit on this side near the plants, so you can look outside? Sometimes a deer will meander by, and there are always squirrels and birds to watch out there. Occasionally, you'll see a couple of big, fat raccoons waddling through the trees over there to the north.

Would you mind praying over the food?

Praise the Lord. Th ank you.

How does everything taste, alright?

A PRICE WORTH PAYING?
[Suffering]
~ 6 ~

You've got to be kidding! You must be a glutton for punishment. I'd think by now you'd be tired of listening to me talk!

Well, you are right about that! They're the only family I know of that's had so many blessings and miracles from God – it's mind boggling. You know, one of the things that really sticks in my mind is all the hard stuff they had to go through before getting a miracle. I wonder how many of us would be willing to pay the price to have those miracles. I'm not saying they were asked and they said, "Oh yes, bring it on." If given the choice, I really don't think they would have chosen all those problems and hard times. What really tweaks my interest are the different steps we have been discussing, the 'steps to a miracle'. At least for me, it isn't worth telling all these great things God has done for them unless God gets '*all*' the praise and glory; unless we can learn something that will help us grow stronger, deeper in the Lord. Without Him, they would have just been another poor family with a lot of problems. Come to think about it, that wouldn't be exactly true.

Had God not intervened, the father, Maurice E., would have stayed dead, which would mean there would not have been the pregnancies, and Mary Helen would not have suffered all those problems from giving birth. There would not have been a "Sonny", Maurice L., or a ConnieJean, and none of their children or grandchildren. The lineage would have just stopped right there with Maurice E. and Mary Helen. Hmm, doesn't that sound like an awful lot of suffering just to continue two lineages into the future?

It makes me wonder if it was important for these two little lives to be brought into this world, what about all those babies aborted, just not wanted. Babies no one felt worth their eff ort and suffering, their inconvenience, to bring into this world. Oh, how it must grieve the heart of God!

In my mind, this takes us right back to the Garden of Eden. What was it Satan said to Eve? "Ye shall not surely die: For God doth know that in the day ye eat thereof, then your eyes shall be opened, and ye shall be as gods, knowing good and evil." Genesis 3:4-5[64] I wonder, 'knowing good and evil' according to whose point of view - God's or Satan's? Have we become as gods in our own eyes, dealing out life and death by the reason and understanding of man, the imaginations of our heart and mind? Have we become "vain in our imaginations and our foolish hearts become darkened . . . professing ourselves to be wise"?[65] I'm reminded the Word of God says ". . . lean not unto thine own understanding"[66]

When a child is aborted, we are not killing one little life. One who may have been God's chosen child to turn us back again to God, or to lead mankind back to love and caring one for another. We are killing generations upon generations of children who collectively may have taught us how to live in peace, one with another, or may have invented something which could have resulted in the survival of millions and millions; maybe even the lives of that mother and father who deemed it unworthy to live.

What a responsibility; a burden to bare! What a fearful thing to stand before an angry God and explain how our life, our comfort, or 'making life easier' was more important than all those lives we ended with just one decision to put ourselves first.

I have a question for you. If you were in God's place, would you have given the father life, knowing all the suffering that would follow that decision? What would YOU do? Would you be more concerned about the suffering, or the lives; what about the miracles and the lives those miracles would touch for years to come? What made them 'chosen' to walk this path of suffering and miracles instead of others we know who are suffering - why them?

Here, once again, my interest is tweaked by the possible "steps to a miracle" we have been discussing. Somehow, I believe some of our answers are in these steps.

Unless we can learn something that will help us grow stronger, deeper, in our Lord; unless we give the Lord all the praise and glory; unless their lives bring faith to hearts; unless souls are brought into the Kingdom of God and bodies healed, then all the suffering would have been for naught. It would have just been suffering!

What do we know about our God? Is He a tyrant who loves to push His weight around and prove He has the upper hand? Is He sadistic, does He love to watch His children suffer? What does His Word say to us? It says He desires to give us food, drink, and clothes to wear.[67] We are His family.[68] He loves little children.[69]

God loves us.[70] He's our God of patience and consolation,[71] our God of hope.[72] He's our Father of mercies and God of comfort,[73] and our God of peace and love.[74] How could we possibly think a God of patience, consolation, hope, mercy, comfort, peace, and love, would just sit idly by, watching His children suffer when we know His Word says, "All things work together for good to them that love God!"[75] Common sense and good reason would tell us, if we are suffering, there is a reason beyond the conclusions of 'He just doesn't care', or 'He's left me to fight this battle all alone'.

His precious Word to us says, "There shall not any man be able to stand before thee all the days of thy life: as I was with Moses, so <u>I will be with thee: I will not fail thee, nor forsake thee.</u> Joshua 1:5[76] "That it might be fulfilled which was spoken by Esaias the prophet, saying, Himself took our infirmities, and bare our sicknesses." Matthew 8:17[77] So, why do we suffer? If God hasn't turned His back on us then why are we suffering?

Two reasons pop readily into my mind, either we are not living according to His Word, will and plan, thus willfully walking away from His love, care, and protection; or, our suffering is for the glory of God. Remember Lazarus? What did our Lord say when his sisters, Martha and Mary, sent word to Jesus that Lazarus (reminding Jesus that Lazarus was "he whom thou lovest") was sick?[78] Why didn't Jesus jump right up and run, or at least walk the approximate eighteen miles fast, and heal Lazarus right on the spot? He could have just spoken the word and Lazarus would have been healed. Why didn't he? What did He say? Jesus said this sickness "...is not unto death, but for the glory of God, that the Son of God might be glorified thereby"[79] Is this then telling us that God is glorified in our sickness? NO! God is not glorified in our sickness; He is glorified in our healing! Then, in my mind, 'if' we are a child of God and living according to His Word, our sicknesses and diseases are to be healed - For the glory of God!!!

Then, why aren't we healed?

There is another reason, which did not 'pop into my mind' quite so readily.

What about Paul? Remember Paul's words in 2 Corinthians "...I will glory of the things which concern mine infirmities..." 2 Corinthians 11:23-31[80] "...yet of myself I will not glory, but in mine infirmities..."[81] *Paul continues to explain... "...<u>my strength is made perfect in weakness</u>... I will rather glory in my infirmities <u>that the power of Christ may rest upon me</u>."[82] He said, "Therefore I take pleasure in infirmities, in reproaches, in necessities, in persecutions, in distresses "for Christ's sake": for <u>when I am weak, then am I strong</u>. 2 Corinthians 12:10[83]

Now we are left with what strongly appears like a contradiction: "God is not glorified in our sickness, He is glorified in our healing!" and "I will ...glory in my infirmities that the power of Christ may rest upon me." When I read this, it leaves me a bit confused, how about you? Should I "seek" healing, or should I "glory" in my infirmities? Let's see what the scripture has to say about this "glorying in infirmities."

First of all, Paul besought the Lord to take away his infirmities; three times he sought the Lord for healing.[84] What changed his heart and mind from seeking healing to glorying in his infirmities [feebleness (of body or mind); by implication malady; moral frailty; disease; infirmity; sickness; weakness[85]]? Paul said "...there was given to me a thorn in the flesh, the messenger of Satan to buffet me, <u>lest I should be exalted above measure.</u> For this thing I besought the Lord thrice, that it might depart from me. And he said unto me, My grace is sufficient for thee: for my strength is made perfect in weakness. Most gladly therefore will I rather glory in my infirmities, that <u>the power of Christ may rest upon me.</u>" 2 Corinthians 12:7-9[86]

There are times we may be called upon to carry our infirmity; when healing would make us susceptible to character flaws, which are not becoming to our Lord, such as pride. If our outreach and service for Christ would be greater with our infirmity than it would be without it, then we, too, should say, "Will I rather glory in my infirmities that the power of Christ may rest upon me."

Now, lest we all rush to thinking we are not to be healed, let me add this one thing. Remember, Paul sought healing three times, until he was told ". . . My grace is sufficient for thee: for my strength is made perfect in weakness."[87] To my recollection, Jesus healed "all" those who were following Him, seeking His teaching and His healing. But Paul was not a "follower", he was a disciple. As a disciple of Christ, he was held to a higher standard; his character must be pure before the Lord "that the power of Christ might rest upon him." He gloried in his "weakness" in the sense that he did not allow himself to become bigheaded and feel important "because of all <u>Christ</u> was <u>doing through him</u>"; he realized he was only human and that Christ was doing the work, not Paul. Often, when we are used mightily by our Lord, we allow ourselves to become self-important in our own eyes. The power and guidance of our Lord may be taken from us if we allow ourselves to become important in our own eyes. Paul chose to *"glory in his infirmities, that he might have the power of Christ in his life"*. When seeking healing, we need to examine our heart, spirit, and lives to determine whether we

Great is Our God... and Greatly to Be Praised!

are living according to God's Word, crying out "Search me, O God, and <u>know my heart: try me,</u> and <u>know my thoughts</u>: And <u>see if there be any wicked way in me</u>, and lead me in the way everlasting." Psalms 139:23-24[88] and tarry for the guidance of the precious Holy Spirit of God until we are either healed or we hear from God.

Again, this brings us back to our possible "steps to a miracle". Are these steps part of our everyday life: are we "living the Word"?

1. Seek the Lord with all your heart and soul, fear the Lord your God and serve Him in truth with all your heart.
2. It isn't the denomination or the building you attend, <u>it's the God you worship and serve and how you seek Him that matters.</u>
3. Be a genuine neighbor and friend.
4. Be a faithful prayer-warrior on the behalf of others.
5. Care and have concern for the needs of others <u>above your own</u> wants and desires.
6. Feed the hungry, give drink to the thirsty, take in the stranger, cloth the naked, visit the sick and those in prison.
7. Endure hardships, pain, and/or suffering while maintaining your deep heart-love for others and their needs.
8. Set your heart to understanding.
9. Be fully persuaded "nothing" can separate you from the love of God.
10. Turn your eyes fully upon Jesus; focus on HIM.
11. Examine your heart, thoughts, and life; from the depth of your soul cry out, *"Search me, Oh God!"*

Before we become too discouraged, thinking there is no way under the sun we'll be able to fulfill all the steps, and struggle forever seeking healing of our bodies; again, remember the words of Paul. "For I know that in me (that is, in my flesh,) dwelleth no good thing: <u>for to will is present</u> with me; but how to perform that which is good I find not. For the good that I would I do not: but the evil which I would not, that I do." Romans 7:18-19[89]

Well then, what are we supposed to do???

"Examine yourselves, whether ye be in the faith; prove your own selves. Know ye not your own selves, how that Jesus Christ is in you . . ." 2 Corinthians 13:5[90] Without Christ and the Holy Spirit dwelling within us, we can do nothing. But, with Christ and the Holy Spirit, we can do all things. "I can do all things *through Christ which strengtheneth me.*" Philippians 4:13[91] "I am *crucified with Christ:* nevertheless I live; yet not I, *but Christ liveth in me:* and the life which I now live in the flesh *I live by the faith* of the Son of God, who loved me, and gave himself for me." Galatians 2:20[92]

Did you catch that?

"Nevertheless I live; yet *not I, but Christ liveth in me*".

The more you live and have your being in the presence and Word of our Lord and Savior, the more that statement will be true in your life. It will become more and more "Christ living in me, not I".

Oh no, I got carried away again, right? It just seems to me we all make everything so hard. The more we dwell in the presence and Word of our Lord, the less we will have to worry about 'being right', 'doing right', or 'saying the right words' for He will be indwelling our hearts and souls, and we will become more like Him.

AND THE MORTARS FELL
[Seth - WWII]
~ 7 ~

I just recently learned another incident involving Dave; do you want to hear it? God is so good to His children! This is almost beyond human belief!

Well, remember I told you how Dave had a Mercantile, a fancy name for a general store? In those days, the customers would come in and hand Dave their list, and Dave would then go around the store collecting all the items on their list. Others would just patiently wait their turn to be "waited on." Does anyone know what it's really like to be "waited on" these days? But when a customer came in who wanted, or needed prayer, the line of customers would patiently wait while Dave went back to the shoe bench in the back of the store and prayed with or for the customer in need. There were even times there would be a small prayer meeting going on back at that old shoe bench.

Seth, Dave's eighth child, two years younger than Maurice, was off in World War II in the European theater. Seth was in the first line of U.S. army soldiers to enter into France. Seth told how the mortars could be heard coming in, and everyone was running with all they had across the open area to get to safety.

For some reason, it seems he was slower than a lot of the others and they were hollering at him, "Seth, run! RUN!"

All of a sudden, he froze in place; he couldn't move! He saw his father, Dave, and a few other men he knew from town kneeling around that old shoe bench praying for him. He couldn't move. He stood there watching them pray for him. It was like he was right there with them; he could name each one and describe what they were wearing as he heard them calling out his name. He felt safe there in the store, back by the old wooden bench.

Then, just as suddenly as he had arrived in his father's familiar store, he was back in the war, on the mortar-whittled field. He no longer saw his father kneeling with the other men. Now freed from his frozen state, he began to move; to run to safety. *Then he saw it*! A big hole, right in front of his feet; a mortar had dropped right in front of him!

I personally don't know anything about war and mortars, except that many lives are lost during those battles. Mortars, so I am told, had pieces of metal shrapnel in them that would furiously fly in all directions; its intent was to kill, maim, or to injure everyone in its path. But this mortar had fallen right in front of his feet, and not only did he not have one single mark or injury, he didn't even know it had fallen. He was at a prayer meeting with his dad and a few men in his hometown!

Oh, PRAISE THE LORD!!!

Seth contacted his father the first chance he had to tell him what had happened, giving him the day and time. Dave told him the exact same men he (Seth) saw were in his shop with him, back at the old shoe bench, praying for Seth at that time, on that very day. Our Lord's precious holy Word says, "A thousand shall fall at thy side, and ten thousand at thy right hand; but it shall not come nigh thee." Psalms 91:7[93] ...it says... "The LORD is thy keeper: the LORD is thy shade upon thy right hand. The sun shall not smite thee by day, nor the moon by night. The LORD shall preserve thee from all evil: he shall preserve thy soul. The LORD shall preserve thy going out and thy coming in from this time forth, and even for evermore." Psalms 121:5-8[94]

GREAT is our GOD, and GREATLY to be PRAISED!!!

There is nothing, absolutely nothing, our God cannot do![95] [96] Why would we even consider walking on our own, doing our own thing, when we have such a loving, caring, heavenly Father? He has everything in His hand as He reaches down for us, everything we need, saying, "Here take my gifts of love, let me take care of you and keep you safe. Take My hand and follow Me." Why do we doubt? Why do we hesitate? No one, NO ONE, loves you like God!

I just don't understand it! If I could come to you with gift s of healing, problem solving, money, protection, warnings of dangers in your path, and anything else you had need of, and told you, "Here take them, these are my free gifts to you," would you not take my gifts and think I was truly wonderful for giving them to you? Wouldn't you love me?

That's exactly what our Lord is doing; He is offering you His service and power, to care for you and to meet all your needs. Doesn't your heart just want to burst forth in song, praises to our Lord! Come on - sing with me.

♪

What a mighty God we serve,
What a mighty God we serve,
Angels bow before Him,
Heaven and earth adore Him,
What a might God we serve.

What a mighty God we serve,
What a mighty God we serve,
Angels bow before Him,
Heaven and earth adore Him,
What a might God we serve.
♪97 98

GLORY! Glory to God most high! Praise His holy, holy, name!!! Hallelujah! Hallelujah!
Oh, hallelujah! . . .

♪

His name is Wonderful,
His name is Wonderful,
His name is Wonderful,
Jesus my Lord.
He is the mighty King,

Master of everything,
His name is Wonderful,
Jesus my Lord.
He's the great Shepherd,
The Rock of all ages,
Almighty God is He,
Bow down before Him,
Love and adore Him,
His name is Wonderful,
Jesus my Lord
♪99

Glory . . . glory . . . **GLORY!**

Great is Our God... and Greatly to Be Praised!

Excuse me, I just have to take a hallelujah break!

♪

Oh, the joy of sins forgiv'n,
Oh, the bliss the blood-washed know,
Oh, the peace akin to Heav'n,
Where the healing waters flow.

Where the healing waters flow,
Where the joys celestial glow,
Oh, there's peace and rest and love,
Where the healing waters flow!

Now with Jesus crucified,
At His feet I'm resting low;
Let me evermore abide
Where the healing waters flow.

Where the healing waters flow,
Where the joys celestial glow,
Oh, there's peace and rest and love,
Where the healing waters flow!

O, this precious, perfect love!
How it keeps the heart aglow,
Streaming from the fount above,
Where the healing waters flow.

Where the healing waters flow,
Where the joys celestial glow,
Oh, there's peace and rest and love,
Where the healing waters flow!

> Oh, to lean on Jesus' breast,
> While the tempests come and go!
> Here is blessed peace and rest,
> Where the healing waters flow.
>
> Where the healing waters flow,
> Where the joys celestial glow,
> Oh, there's peace and rest and love,
> Where the healing waters flow!
>
> Cleansed from every sin and stain,
> Whiter than the driven snow,
> Now I sing my sweet refrain,
> Where the healing waters flow.
>
> Where the healing waters flow,
> Where the joys celestial glow,
> Oh, there's peace and rest and love,
> Where the healing waters flow!
>
> ♪100

Doesn't your heart just want to burst for joy, so full of His wondrous love! Just think of it, first he saves us from our spiritual death by taking on all our sins and becoming our sacrifice; then, He walks with us and talks with us by His Spirit to guide us into all truth, and He fights our battles. But that's not all, He also meets our mental, emotional, and physical needs, too! Oh yes, I forgot, and our financial needs, too! Just tell me, what doesn't our Lord do for us?

And all He asks is, "Love Me." What a wondrous God we serve! Oh my, I'm so full of His blessed, precious presence!

LED BY A CHILD
[Danger!]
8

Our Lord is like the greatest, most loving parent anyone could even imagine. He loves us even when we are at our worst; even before we know Him as our heavenly Father and we've turned our backs on Him; even when we think we know what's right or best and think our reason and logic are so superior to His.

Oh, you say, "I would never think that way, I know better than that! I'd never compare my reasoning ability and understanding with His."

Really! Never? What are we really saying when we choose to do what "we" want to do, and do it "our way". Isn't that questioning His superior knowledge, reasoning, and coming to the decision "we know best"?

I honestly believe when our heavenly Father watches us and interacts with us some days, He must really laugh. We think we know so much! We think we can please our Lord by following our own ideas and reasoning. You know, as adults we aren't so much different than little Sonny and ConnieJean were at the ages of four and three.

Don't believe me? Okay, let me tell you a couple little stories; just see if you can't see yourself in there somewhere.

Sonny was growing into a jolly, really good-natured, little boy, who appeared, except for his one eye damaged during childbirth, to be as normal as any other child, with maybe a tad more inquisitiveness about him. He also slid into the role of a child problem-solver. Hmm, did you ever know anyone who knew how to solve everybody's problems – who knew what everyone should or shouldn't do?

There are two stories I recall hearing about Sonny in his pre-school years, when he would 'slip away' unnoticed to 'help daddy'. I suppose his mommy and daddy were busy doing all the things mommies and daddies have to do, like laundry and mowing the yard, I don't know. But Sonny seemed to know when he could take off walking and not be noticed for a little while. He wasn't really being naughty; he just wanted to help his daddy.

One time, while joking around and playing with him, Maurice said, "Whenever you get any money, bring it home to Daddy, Daddy needs all the money he can get." Later that day, Sonny slipped away unnoticed, making his way up the street, door-by-door, collecting a penny here and a nickel there. He finally made his way up town - a whole four blocks! I'm sure he felt really big, going all the way to town by himself.

Sonny returned with a handful of coins which he handed to his daddy, beaming from ear to ear. Sonny had gone down the street and into town, a few blocks away from home, telling everyone that his daddy needed money (much to the embarrassment of his daddy).

In those days, no one had to worry about your neighbor or the stranger passing through. Everyone in town was either family or friends, and they all looked out for each other. Now I'm not saying a mother and father's heart wouldn't go into a panic mode if they couldn't find their little one, or that they wouldn't go scurrying around looking for their precious child, wondering if he/she was alright - if he/she was lost. But, you didn't have to be afraid of what a neighbor or stranger 'might do' to your little one; only that they had strayed off and gotten lost or somehow hurt themselves. Oh, how things have changed. How sad it is that our little ones cannot know 'trust' and 'innocence' and good 'ole 'naiveté' the way we did (at least I did) growing up. The many things we didn't know, and didn't need to know, and weren't afraid of, in those 'good old days'; but today our children must learn to be sober, watchful, temperate, vigilant, suspecting possible harm to come like a prowling, roaring lion, seeking whom he may devour, 1 Peter 5:8[101], crouched behind every corner.

Mom, dad, what have we allowed to creep into our world, into the lives of our little ones, during our watch? Have we turned our eyes away from God and allowed evil to slip in the back door; into our world, into our towns, into our very homes? It's not too late! It's not too late for us, for our little ones - our sons and daughters, our grandchildren, and great grandchildren - *if* we truly, sincerely turn back to God and His love and mercy for all! 1 Chronicles 7:14[102] We can rid ourselves and our children of the prowling, roaring evil that stalks our streets *if* we humbly, sincerely, return to God, prayer, and His guidance; God's Holy Word. God's Spirit cries out to one and all, "Come home; return to your God, to the One who desires to love and protect you from the evil of this world." "Suffer the little children to come unto me and forbid them not" Matthew 19:14, Mark 10:14, Luke 18:16[103] Come home."

You know, there is another lesson we can learn from Sonny's 'well meaning'; his heart was in the right place. Sonny-boy, who really only heard, 'daddy needs all the money he can get,' sort of reminds me of those of us who don't 'get the whole story'; our minds are too busy to listen to the whole conversation and we think we've 'heard enough' - all we need to know. Now that's fine with little children, maybe a little embarrassing from time to time, as they believe they know what's happening or needed without really listening to the whole story. Even as children can get themselves into a predicament by only knowing half the truth or story, we adults can really get ourselves into trouble up to our necks, and then some. Listening with a double mind, half listening and half off somewhere else, is like the game teachers used to play in elementary classrooms. The teacher whispers something to one child, who whispers it to another, and another, and another. Remember what happened? Sometimes the story the last child heard was nothing like the story the teacher told the first child. Somehow, it just keeps "evolving" into a variation of the truth. When we "half listen" to the things people are telling us, our stories tend to end up being "half-truths" we forward on to others.

But, Sonny meant well! His daddy needed money, and he went out and got his daddy some money.

Another time, I heard Maurice was out in the garden digging potatoes, sweat dripping from his face. He wiped the sweat off his brow with the sleeve of his right arm while leaning on his shovel, and commented, "I sure could use some help digging up all these potatoes."

Sometimes, the 'talkers' aren't really listening to what they're saying or keeping in mind who they are saying it to. Guess you could call them 'lazy talkers'. These kind of 'talkers' just open their mouths and let 'er fly! Sometimes joking, but forgetting to let the listener in on that little fact.

So, what happened in our little story?

This time Sonny made it all the way to grandpa's house on the other side of town and across the railroad tracks, picking up a couple men along the way, saying daddy needed help; so the men, and grandpa with his little "Chunny Man" and shovels in hand, walked back home to help his daddy dig potatoes.

He meant well.

They really had to watch what they said around him, or he'd be off on a mission to "fix it."

Remember Seth in the battlefield? Well, that same heavenly Father was right there with little Sonny, protecting him from all the dangers that could have befallen a little four year-old boy. We don't have to be in a battle field. In this day and age, we live in a war zone right here on the streets and playgrounds of our home towns; Satan's influences are everywhere 'seeking whom he may devour'.[104] It doesn't matter if we are living in a peaceful little rural town, or in the biggest, noisiest, metropolitan city in the world, our heavenly Father is there, watching out for us, placing His mighty hand of protection between us and the mortars of the devil. We have the most gracious heavenly Father constantly watching out for us, you, and me. One who is always there to protect us from the mortars and shrapnel of life; but He also protects us from ourselves, our own mistakes, and deeds of immaturity.

What a gracious God we serve!

I'm also reminded that behind our Lord's mighty hand of protection was a man named Dave and some faithful prayer warriors. Are you; am I, one of those faithful prayer warriors? A prayer warrior who will drop anything, everything, no matter whether I'm home alone or out in public?

Someone's life may rest on your immediate intercession on their behalf. What child or teenager will be saved from danger and harm, what soul on the brink of death will reach out to God because *you* immediately obeyed the Spirit's call to prayer?

Oh my God, help me to realize the seriousness of each and every call to prayer by Your precious Holy Spirit! Oh, my most precious Lord, help me, by Your Spirit, to immediately obey Your Spirit's call, to listen intently for your call! Lord, let me not let down one person, child, or one soul in need; Lord, let no man suffer because I have neglected so great a call to pray. Oh my Lord, my God, make me an instrument of your healing and comfort! Help me. Help me always to hear and obey your voice!

I know we don't like the feeling of being compared to a little four year-old; but no matter how old we become, we can always learn from a child. The word of God says, "Suffer the little children to come unto me, and forbid them not: for of such is the kingdom of God. Verily I say unto you, Whosoever shall not receive the kingdom of God as a little child, he shall not enter therein." Mark 10:14-15[105] The more we 'truly' watch and learn from a little child, the closer we will become the "children of God".

Looking at the lives of Sonny and ConnieJean, I believe it is not 'what' the little child does that we are to emulate, but 'why' they do what they do - their sweet innocence; their sincerity of heart.

Oh, Sonny didn't save all his good deeds for his daddy. It was said if he was offered anything, coins or sweet treats for instance, he would refuse to accept it unless there was enough for his "sissy", too. He even carried that to the extent that if she was punished for something, he would cry and insist he should be punished too. Or when she had to be given something she didn't want, like castor oil, he would insist he had to have some, too.

I remember Mary Helen telling about the first time she gave ConnieJean castor oil; she said Sonny fussed and insisted if "sissy" had to take it he did, too. After all, they were the same, 'twins in two batches'. So, knowing it wouldn't hurt him, she gave Sonny a little, too. She said the kids began gagging, both of them. So thinking it would help, she rushed into the kitchen and grabbed some soda crackers, giving them each a cracker to eat. The cracker gummed up with the castor oil; she said it was a real gagging mess!

Laughing, Mary Helen said, "It was so funny, I couldn't help but laugh; they just stood there looking at each other, their little faces all twisted in disdain and nausea, gagging." Mary Helen said she never, ever gave them castor oil again!

There are just some times, due to our immaturity in the Lord, we 'don't like', or we 'disagree' with something those in authority have decided to do. We step in and involve ourselves in situations which we really do not belong in, thinking we are right and showing our support for the one being corrected or treated in a way we "feel" is wrong. Just like Sonny and ConnieJean, sometimes these times become disdainful and unpleasant; but there are times when immature interference can cause spiritual suffering, pain, and rejection of one's beliefs in God and His Word.

Okay, now you're saying, "What in the world does she want us to do? First, she says 'be as little children.' Then she tells us we are 'not to be immature like little children'. Can't she make up her mind?"

Let me explain. I am saying we are all to become sweet, innocent, and trusting as a little child in our spirit toward our heavenly Father, with a heart to please Him; but we are to mature in love and wisdom through prayer and the reading and preaching of God's holy word and grow toward perfection in Him. Actually, one might think this is a spectacular juggling act, balancing the innocence and trust of a little child, and the mind and intellect of a mature adult. And ***it is***, by ourselves. In our own strength and wisdom it is impossible, but, with God's precious Spirit to help and guide you through the labyrinths and mazes of this school called 'life', we can become 'more than conquerors'.

Paul tells us, "Who shall separate us from the love of Christ? Shall tribulation, or distress, or persecution, or famine, or nakedness, or peril, or sword? As it is written, for thy sake we are killed all the day long; we are accounted as sheep for the slaughter. Nay, in all these things we are more than conquerors through him that loved us. For I am persuaded, that neither death, nor life, nor angels, nor principalities, nor powers, nor things present, nor things to come, nor height, nor depth, nor any other creature, shall be able to separate us from the love of God, which is in Christ Jesus our Lord." Romans 8:35-39[106] Remember what the scripture mentioned earlier? "But Jesus beheld them, and said unto them, With men this is impossible; but with God all things are possible." Matthew 19:26[107] "If thou canst believe, all things are possible to him that believeth."

Mark 9:23[108] "And Jesus looking upon them saith, With men it is impossible, but not with God: for with God all things are possible." Mark 10:27[109]

Okay, let me tell you another one about 'a little child'. Th is is about the time ConnieJean almost killed her daddy.

ConnieJean was given quiet things to do to occupy her time while she was confined to the sofa for health reasons. She had coloring books and colors; little girl stitching projects with a big, fat, dull embroidery needle; kittens crawling all over her and lying with her (she loved the kittens, they were her best friends and companions!); 'follow the dot' books; paper doll books; and a ball and jacks set she could play with while sitting quietly on the floor.

One day she had been working studiously on a stitching project while her daddy sat in a nearby chair reading the paper. He was 'always reading the paper', especially if anyone came to their house. Mary Helen said he would hide behind the paper until the visitor left their home, even family members. He was so shy.

Anyway, ConnieJean liked what she had done and got up to show it to her daddy, but he just kept reading the paper. So she crawled up on the left arm of the overstuffed chair and tried to get his attention, but decided since he was busy she would take another stitch or two. She took one stitch, two stitches, then, when she took the third stitch the needle stuck in the cloth. She tugged and tugged as best she could in her weakened condition, but it just didn't want to come out. So, she grabbed the needle as far down as she could next to the fabric and gave it all her strength and yanked - it came out!

But, her daddy grabbed his left temple in pain; the end of the needle had stuck in Maurice's temple. He pulled and tugged trying to get the needle out of his head, but couldn't; it was too deep. He called Mary Helen to come over and pull it out. She pulled on it, but she couldn't get it out. Maurice told Mary Helen to go get a pair of pliers out of his toolbox to pull it out. After retrieving the pliers, she tugged and tugged but the needle just would not come out. About that time, Seth stopped by for a visit, so Maurice asked him to pull out the needle. He took the pliers and cautiously but firmly pulled on the needle, several times, but it would not come out. I was told Maurice finally went into the bedroom alone with the pliers in hand and shut the door.

Either I can't remember, or I wasn't told how long Maurice was in that bedroom, but when he came out, the needle was out of his head. No one said if there were any lasting effects from carrying that needle around stuck in his head for hours and hours that day, but it sure couldn't have felt very good!

Do you suppose God helped him take out the needle? It was said, after he came out of that bedroom, he went about his normal routine as though nothing had happened.

Oh, the trouble little innocent hands can get into! My advice, "beware of little girls carrying needles!"

I can just hear you now, saying what in the world does this have to do with our walk in Christ? Well, as 'little children', we often reap consequences from 'well meaning' but unthought out actions; we cannot always know what the result of our actions will be. Folks, we make mistakes, sometimes they are little mistakes of little importance, but sometimes it's a 'granddaddy' of a mistake, with tremendous consequences to ourselves and/or others. This is an example where our Lord would have us mature and grow in understanding and knowledge, to exercise our God-given oneness with His Spirit to have child-like trust to be led into His paths of righteousness. Of course, here I am speaking of our lives in our Lord, and our walk in the precious Holy Spirit. All kinds of things enter the life of a child of God. We call them tests, trials, and tribulations; each of which provides us with an open door to use the knowledge, understanding, and wisdom thus learned as we've walked this path in our Lord, or to rest in obedience as we follow the gentle bidding of our precious Holy Spirit teacher and guide. These days, I am repeatedly reminded of the scripture that says, "And he that searcheth the hearts knoweth what is the mind of the Spirit, because he maketh intercession for the saints according to the will of God. And we know that all things work together for good to them that love God, to them who are the called according to his purpose." Romans 8:27-28[110]

I truly believe with all my heart, we have allowed ourselves to be drawn, by the understanding and reasoning of this world, to look upon the gifts of opportunity and training as tests, trials, and tribulations. A test to one man is a challenge to another. It's all in how you look at things; your outlook will determine how you will approach and go through a situation, an open door, which has been placed before you. Do we really, really believe that ". . .*God is able to make all grace abound toward you; that ye, always having all sufficiency in all things, may abound to every good work*:" 2 Corinthians 9:8[111]

Have you ever known a "professional student"? Are you a professional student in God's word and walk in the Spirit? Okay, this is not a dictionary definition of a professional student, I grant you. But this is what I see when I look at a person who is referred to as a professional student; they do not get all bogged down with fear, anxiety, and discouragement, as each new 'class' becomes a step of growth and learning. The professional student excitedly takes on the challenge of a new class (giving it their best, I might add) with an eye looking ahead to the next, more challenging class they will then be qualified to take. Those I have known during my life have started talking about and planning the next class within a week or two of the current class they are taking, eager to learn and grow. How many of us are eager, and take on each new 'training of our Lord' with anticipation and determination to learn as much as possible, as quickly as possible, to become the best in our 'field' serving our Lord?

There's another thought that enters my mind about ConnieJean's story, the fact she chose to move 'before' the situation was open to her. Thinking it was somehow 'better' to wait sitting on the arm of her daddy's chair rather than remain on the sofa, she took it upon herself to reposition herself. Maybe she was thinking only about herself. Maybe she just wanted to be near her daddy, or just wanted him to like what she'd done, or wanted him to think she had done a great job, do you suppose? Maybe she just wasn't thinking. What I see here appears to be all about what 'she wanted', all about 'her' with no thought of anything else at the time. She meant well; she meant no harm.

How many times in our Christian walk, do we 'reposition' ourselves, without our precious Holy Spirit's guidance and preparation opening the doors before us? In our child-like thinking, we decide 'I'd like', 'I think', 'I believe', 'I want', etc, etc. We decide something should be done a 'better' way or a 'different' way, or if we reposition ourselves maybe, just maybe, we will be recognized as being really good or great: important. Are we longing for the attention or lime light of someone at our place of work or our church? When we take it upon ourselves to reposition ourselves without our precious guide's preparation and guidance, we are opening the doors for harm to ourselves and/or others. Often, the opposite of those things we longed for or desired is the harvest of our actions. ConnieJean did not get the accolades and attention she wanted and repositioned herself to receive; she had caused so much damage, confusion, and worry, that all her wants, hopes, and goals were lost in the storm she had caused; 'she' was lost in a storm of her own making. When we take steps to do things when we want or our way without waiting for the Lord's will and timing, we, too, will be lost in the storm it creates. Instead of pleasing our heavenly Father, we will berth a storm of confusion and pain.

As parents, one of the greatest gifts we can give our children is the gift of learning to listen and obey. When a child learns to listen and obey their father and mother, they will then find it easier to obey those in authority over them, and even more importantly, they will learn how to listen and obey the Spirit of their great and loving heavenly Father. They will become followers (of our Lord) and not self-centered doers. Have we taught our children well, by instruction or example? Have we, ourselves, learned the lesson and need of 'following'?

ConnieJean wasn't a bad girl, she was just a little child who did it 'her way' and caused destruction and pain. What kind of a Christ-child am I? What kind of a Christ-child are you? When our heavenly Father may seem to be quiet and inattentive, or a little slow, busying Himself with other matters or plans, tell me, what are we doing? Waiting and growing, or repositioning?

"And you will again give ear to the voice of the Lord, and do all his orders which I have given you today. And the Lord your God will make you fertile in all good things, blessing the work of your hands, and the fruit of your body, and the fruit of your cattle, and the fruit of your land: for the Lord will have joy in you, as he had in your fathers: If you give ear to the voice of the Lord your God, keeping his orders and his laws which are recorded in this book of the law, and turning to the Lord your God with all your heart and with all your soul." Deuteronomy 30:8-10 (BBE)[112]

Well, are you up to hearing a couple more stories, the continuing saga of Sonny and ConnieJean? Or, is it getting too late?

There are two or three really short ones I'd like to tell you, if you'd care to hear them. It just seems to me Sonny and ConnieJean at this age are so representative of the kind of childlike Christians most of us are today. These Christians need to grow and mature into a 'child-like' Christian who listens to the voice of God and the blessed Holy Spirit, and who weighs everything in light of God's word and guidance 'before' they act. It seems to me, we are all 'child-like' in our walk with the Lord, but we can either be like the child who is obedient and trusting or we can be like the child who is immature and foolish. Which are we?

We can learn so much about our Christian walk if we just watch children and allow the blessed Holy Spirit to open our eyes and understanding, to reveal our spiritual immaturity to us through the 'little-child'. The worst and the best of what we can be in the Lord can be seen through that innocent little child.

Okay, you're sure you have the time?

Great is Our God... and Greatly to Be Praised!

Seth (1919-1985) and Helen (Lower/1921-1966) Marquart

Well, one of the stories is about the time when Mary Helen and Helen, Seth's wife, found a perfectly good Jenny Lynn bed headboard, or was it given to Mary Helen, I'm not sure. I seem to recall the headboard had been painted with several layers of paint. Looking around, they found the perfect spot to work on it, and lovingly set the headboard up against the back of the house with an old, thin blanket behind it so as to protect this precious treasure, and proceeded to work diligently removing all the old paint. It wasn't as easy as one might think it would be. The paint job wasn't the best they had ever seen; resulting in some really thick areas. But, they set their minds to doing it, and do it they would; besides they always had such great times when they were together, and this was a great excuse. It was decided they would don some old clothes first thing in the morning and start wiping it down with turpentine to see if it would remove the excess paint. Of course a good, hot cup of coffee would be needed to start the day. You can't just dive into work like that, it must be eased into. After a cup, well, knowing those two maybe two, they were off to the races; paint removal race that is. One on each side of the headboard, they worked and laughed the day away until they had to rush in order to get the day's work done before their men arrived. Carefully, they covered this gem they envisioned in their minds, and retreated each to their own home to 'pick up' the house and get supper going on the stove.

The next day, they decided to turn their schedule the other way around, so they hurriedly 'picked up' their houses and prepared their meals for that night. Then it was back to Mary Helen's kitchen for that hot cup of coffee and deciding just how much they would get done that day. They bounced around the idea that maybe, just maybe, they'd be able to get all the paint off that day. Finishing their coffee, they went out, uncovered their prize, and began working. Just like a potter, or a Michael Angelo, each knew the beauty they were trying to coax forth out of that old headboard; the deep rich color of the wood and beautiful grain, it would be their work of art.

Reluctantly, they decided they had to quit again for the night, their men would be coming home soon and Helen lived four blocks away; she had to have time to get back home and freshen up. They would surely complete their masterpiece tomorrow. Again, they carefully covered up the headboard,

Great is Our God... and Greatly to Be Praised!

admiring how good it was looking. Tomorrow they would get down into the little lines and grooves of the design; they didn't want one speck of that old paint left on their headboard.

You know, I wonder if they had some kind of share-plan for their joint endeavor, maybe one would get it for a month or two, maybe six, then it would be the other one's turn. Never heard of any such plan, but I sure wouldn't want to be the one going home empty handed after all that work, would you?

They were excited, this would be the day they finished it. This time it was a first-thing-in- the-morning gathering in that little kitchen, right after the men left for work, and it was a quick inhaling of their coffee before they were out back again unveiling their soon-to-be-completed "tour de force". They were riding an effervescent high; laughing, joking, and parading in front of it, giving it a sharp-eyed inspection for any one speck of paint. They dared there to be even one single, miniscule speck on their wooden canvas.

It was done, completed! Finally, it was back to all the splendor and beauty they had known was hidden down deep inside. Standing there gazing for several minutes, only to step up and check it for a speck or ding, then smiling widely, step back and say, "Nope, it was just a reflection." After some time passed, Mary Helen and Helen decided it was time to celebrate their great work with another cup of coffee, so into the house they went.

Do you hear that music playing in the far distance? You know; the kind you hear on TV or at a movie, just before the monster creeps out of the deep, dark woods?

Where are they? Those two "Dennis the Menaces", Sonny & ConnieJean, they've sure been quiet as a mouse the last few days, haven't they?

While Mary Helen and Helen were celebrating in the kitchen, Sonny had a wonderful idea.

Oh, it had to be Sonny, he was the one who always had ideas and ConnieJean followed him around like he was a pied piper or something; besides, sweet, little, innocent ConnieJean could never come up with such a plan as this, could she?

She can't remember, and they can't tell!

She followed Sonny out through the back yard and into the little shed on the northeast corner of the lot; it was dark in there, really dark. Next, they were out in the bright sunlight again, it almost hurt her eyes after being in that dark shed. Sonny's hands were full and he handed his little sissy some things to carry; soft on one end and a handle on the other; paint brushes!

They would 'help' mommy with her work on her new bed, and surprise her. The brush was so big and heavy ConnieJean could barely hold it up. In fact, it kept falling to one side or the other, even two-handed. Hurry, hurry, surprise mommy!

Mary Helen and Helen just had to come back out and admire their work - it was so beautiful. They would carry it into the house and put it in the bedroom. It would really look great!

When they came out of the house, they slapped their hands over their mouths and almost fell to their knees in shock. The beautiful Jenny Lynn headboard was now the most horrible, icky green anyone could have imagined; thick green globs of paint all over their newly restored Jenny Lynn bed!

Standing, with wet brushes in hand and paint all over them, Sonny and ConnieJean said, "We made it beautiful for you, Mommy", faces beaming with pride. They meant well!

I'm sure Mary Helen and Helen cried a little inside, all that work, all that time spent on every little detail! Then looking at the two beaming, green imps, they began to laugh; those two ladies could always find something to laugh about. They remembered how much fun they had doing the bed together, and all the laughing they'd done while they were working on it. Looking at each other, they both began to shake their heads in a horizontal motion and laugh. Almost simultaneously, they said, "NO, I'm not doing it again!" Resigning themselves to the idea, 'guess it just wasn't supposed to be,' they packed up the once-beautiful Jenny Lynn headboard and took it to the dump. Maybe someone else would see it there, see its hidden beauty, and decide to restore it.

Were they little angels or what? NO, not the women; I'm talking about the two little kids.

Oh, I've got another one for you; last one.

I was told one day Mary Helen went outside to hang her freshly washed clothes on the line in the bright sunshine, the fresh clean scent of sun-dried clothes always lifted her spirits a bit. There was the warm sunshine, the beautiful aroma of flowers drifting across the air, and birds' chirping in the trees nearby; it was a good day. She walked slowly back into the house taking in as much of the outdoors as she could.

***"WHAT ... WHAT* IS THAT!**," she exclaimed as she walked over to see red 'stuff' all over her freshly mopped floors. CATSUP! CATSUP and SUGAR! She always kept their little home clean, even with two 'rag-a-muffins' running around the house. Dare I say two little imps! I don't think anyone ever knew why or what they thought they were doing, but Sonny, in the lead with a bottle of catsup, and ConnieJean pulling up the rear with the sugar, walked from the kitchen to the black pot belly stove room, to the downstairs bedroom, through the bathroom, and then back into the kitchen. Around and around the circle of rooms they went leaving a trail of catsup and sugar.

It was hard work to get that sugar right on top of the red catsup, the bag of sugar was so heavy for a frail little girl to carry, but she managed; and around and around they went.

I really don't know what they thought they were doing, but Mary Helen sure had a surprise when she came back into the house!

And you thought **YOU** had a hard time raising YOUR KIDS!

Immature, child-like individuals seem to always 'mean well'; just like Sonny and ConnieJean, they don't see the potential for damage and harm. Seeing only with tunnel vision what they want or what they want to do, not the outcome of their actions.

'2' ... '4' ... '6 EEE'
[As a Little Child]
~ 9 ~

Do you remember the scripture in Isaiah, chapter eleven, where it says, "And a little child shall lead them".[113] Did you ever wonder why those animals were mentioned, and not others? Or why it lists both domestic and wild animals, pairing them together? Could it be trying to show us the worst and best of mankind, telling us a 'child-like', 'Christ-like' person is to become their guide to Him?

What in the world does it mean; a child-like Sonny or ConnieJean, always into mischief or doing crazy things but 'meaning well'?

This scripture speaks of a wolf, lamb, leopard, kid, calf, lion, and fatling. Let's see what these animals can show us about human nature.

The first grouping is the wolf and a lamb; what can we learn from them? Well, wolves like to run in packs, they intimidate and pursue their prey like a single-minded mob, attacking from all directions, furiously ripping apart its defenseless foe. Wolves are vicious as they rip and tear at their prey from every side. Often, even when you can't see them, you know wolves are in the area by their haunting howls of intimidation and threats.

Some people, like these wolves, form groups or clicks attacking anyone who doesn't look, act, or believe as they do; furiously ripping apart their beliefs, values, or way of life. These wolves seem to be heard constantly barking out 'their ideas' and growling, 'it isn't fair' or 'I don't have what they have' or 'I don't get as much as they do'; howling, barking and growling about 'their rights'. They are never satisfied and always on the prowl. Do you know anybody like this?

Now the lamb, on the other hand, likes to flock together, to congregate in a group; but unlike the wolf, the lamb is gathering for protection from its predator. You know the old adage, 'there's comfort in numbers'?

This peaceful, non-threatening lamb seeks to avoid all threats of danger and poses no harm. He instinctively follows the leader; staying near, posing no challenge or threat to others. These meek little lambs are often found in unfenced pastures due to their desire to stay near the family/flock, and they are extremely food-oriented, following a food source or even soliciting food; willing followers, especially for those carrying a bucket full of promises to feast on later. Gifted with good, sensitive hearing, a very good sense of smell, and excellent peripheral vision of 270° to 320° allowing them to see behind themselves without turning their heads; their primary defense is to run away, preferably uphill and out into the light. As gentle and gifted as they are, they do have one serious fault, poor depth perception, causing them to bulk and run from shadows and dips in the ground in front of them. They can hear and see (hind sight) very well, but lack

Great is Our God... and Greatly to Be Praised!

the perception or understanding to choose their path wisely. Fearful and skittish, they run from imagined enemies. They are free, in reality, with no fences or boundaries to fetter them in any way, but they are bound by their inner instinct and desire to be part of the group. Isaiah 11:6 states, "the wolf also shall dwell with the lamb".[114]

Well, what do these two animals have in common? From what I can see, they basically have one thing in common, although for vastly different reasons; they both like traveling in groups. The wolf employs the pack mentality to overpower and kill, whereas the lamb feels safer from its predators by being in a group. Aside from this one factor, I find these two to be complete opposites.

<u>Wolf</u>	<u>Lamb</u>
Hunter	Prey
Attacks	Runs from confrontation
Aggressive	Meek
Agitated	Calm
Loud	Quiet
Overpowers	Follows
Takes food	Eats what is provided

Yet we are told in the scripture these two will dwell together. Just think of it, the predator and the prey dwelling together.

Next, we have the leopard and the kid, young goat, paired together stating "... the leopard shall lie down with the kid ..."[115] Okay, let's see what we can find out about these two.

Leopards, powerful swimmers and very agile, can run over thirty-six miles per hour, leap twenty feet, and jump up to 9.8 feet in the air. They are climbing cats, dragging their kill up in trees and resting on tree branches. Leopards like to hunt their prey best between sunset and sunrise and they stalk their prey silently, making a quick kill with a single bite to the throat. They're so strong they can kill prey three times their own size and drag it up in a tree. The leopard is a solitary cat, a loner, and interactions between other cats appear to be infrequent, aside from mating.

The leopards of this world are powerful climbers, those who are the fastest and best, physically and mentally, those who quickly excel above all those around them; dragging the 'useful' prey along with them to the top, only to devour and discard them when they are no longer useful. Quietly sizing up their target, they leap with a powerful bite to their most vulnerable weakness, overcoming all resistance and personal standards, quickly killing the prey's determination and will power. Like night-life seekers, these leopards come out in the dark of night to stalk out one to meet its mating needs and then leaves to continue its life of self-absorbed seclusion. Th is cat's only interests and/or concerns are satisfying its own immediate wants and desires; it has no concern for another of its own species, or any other.

As for the Kid, I didn't really find much on the 'young' goat; everything I saw was about a mature goat. Goats are extremely intelligent and curious, and unlike the lamb, are known for escaping their pens. Since they are very intelligent, once a goat has figured out how to escape its boundaries by pushing a section of fence over or down, or climbing over it, the goat will do so repeatedly. Being very coordinated, they can climb and hold their balance in the most precarious places; they are known to climb leaning trees bowed by wind or erosion. Goats make a bleating sound and establish dominance in the flock sometimes through head butting. I would think this young kid would have basically the same traits as his adult counterpart, except generously seasoned with the playfulness and inattention of youth.

The young 'kid' reminds me of Sonny; climbing out of the upstairs window, going over the roof, and shimmying down a tree. As a youth, he could always find a way out that appeared to be far more interesting than walking down the steps to the first floor and out the back door. After all, what challenge would that be for his very curious and intelligent mind!

And the 'head butting' for dominance wasn't exactly a characteristic lost on him either, except his head butting was more like 'brain butting', vying for the mental 'top dog' position. Oh, do you remember, this boy was supposed to be a mental vegetable. Just like the 'kid', Sonny never had to figure out the same thing twice!

In some ways, I believe this to be the weirdest pairing of all; one of the swiftest, strongest, most agile - a powerful silent killer - paired with an innocent, unaware, little kid. In the animal world, this would be like a pedophile lying next to an innocent, trusting, little child; the most dangerous predator and the most innocent, side-by-side.

We have one more grouping left in this scripture, it says "... the calf and the young lion and the fatling together..."[116]

A calf, or young bull, of one year-old is noted in Leviticus, as the sacrifice used for the priests' sin offering at the door of the tent of meeting, and the fatling is a young calf or lamb purposely grown to be a sacrificial offering; but why insert the young lion into this grouping?

May I suggest this is representative of our children and their little friends? Some will eventually sacrifice their lives, serving God in the service of others. Some are raised from birth to serve in the Temple, taught and trained in the ways and things of our Lord. But there are those among a child's friends and acquaintances who will grow up as little lions, challenging, fighting. But now, at this very young age, they are all innocent and trainable; with great potential to do good.

Lions are inactive for about twenty hours per day; activity generally peaks after dust with periods of socializing and grooming, most often hunting around dawn. They spend about two hours per day walking and fifty minutes per day eating. The Lionesses do most of the killing due to the lions being encumbered by the heavy and conspicuous mane, which causes overheating during exertion. However, nearby males have a tendency to dominate the kill once the lionesses have succeeded, sharing excess food with the cubs and only reluctantly with the lionesses. Both males and females defend the pride (family). Young males around two or three years old are forced out of the pride to fend for themselves. Membership in the pride depends on births and deaths; the females will not tolerate an outside female to enter the pride.

Left to his fleshly instincts, the young lion will grow up to be one of the beautiful strutting kings of this world's jungles, the godfather of his pride. He often sits on the sidelines while others do the 'dirty work' of killing the prey, which he quickly takes charge of and satisfies his need for ownership, dominance, and hunger. After he is fully satiated, this king will share his scraps with the cubs (the weak, non-threatening)

Great is Our God... and Greatly to Be Praised!

and reluctantly with those proving their strengths, abilities, and instincts (gifts), which ultimately provided for him.

Isn't it strange, the word of God says "... a little child shall lead them"?[117] The pure, innocent child of God filled with trust and obedience to God's word and His precious Holy Spirit shall not fall prey to the predators of this world; they shall be led into peaceful cohabitation by the 'little child'.

Have you ever noticed how the presence of a sweet, innocent, little child can bring calm and peace into a room full of agitated, on-edge adults; all it takes is just one, sweet-spirited, little child.

Remember Mark 10:14-15[118] where it says if we do not receive the kingdom of God as a 'little child', we will not be allowed to enter into heaven? That means we must become pure and innocent through Christ, and as trusting and obedient of God's word and His precious Holy Spirit as a little child. And, when we have done so, we are to lead, show the predators of this world the way to God's peace and cohabitation 'by our example'. Are we that example today in our daily lives? Are we timid or hiding in fear? Or, obediently leading the way to God?

Heavenly Father, by your precious Holy Spirit and Holy Word of God, teach me to become a faithful "little child" living in your word and walking in your precious Holy Spirit. Cleanse me Lord from all uncleanness and sin, all unrighteousness; oh my Lord and my God, make me a pure and holy sacrifice that I might enter into your courts, your presence, on behalf of those in this world who know you not. Father, that I might be acceptable through your Son; an acceptable vessel to bring the needs of your people before you. Oh Father, that I might enter your inner court, the holy of holies, and touch the heart of God with the needs of your children!

I sincerely believe we are often not receiving those things we come into His presence and ask for, because we are coming into his courts with soiled hands and unrighteous hearts and minds. Only the righteous, the clean, those made perfect (mature) in Christ are received into the inner, most holy courts of our Father, that place where prayers are heard and needs are met. My heart cries out, *"Search me, O God, and know my heart: try me, and know my thoughts: And see if there be any wicked way in me, and lead me in the way everlasting."* Psalms 139:23-24[119]

Oh Father, that I might be found acceptable to enter your inner courts; a sacrifice, broken and humble in spirit." Only the young (child-like), perfect (mature), sacrifice could be brought to the door of the tent of meeting, and only on it could the sins and guilt of God's people be symbolically transferred and brought before Jehovah, the Lord God almighty. It was a fearful thing to enter His temple unworthily, to eat of His holy offerings unworthily, to touch that which was holy, unworthily. We must first cleanse our hearts and souls before we come before Jehovah, our God. He deserves - requires - no less of us!

"Ye ask, and receive not, because ye ask amiss..." James 4:3[120]

May I suggest that one of the ways we ask 'amiss' is by coming before our Lord in unrighteousness. We are instructed "Draw nigh to God, and he will draw nigh to you. Cleanse your hands, ye sinners; and purify your hearts, ye double minded. Be afflicted, and mourn, and weep: let your laughter be turned to mourning, and your joy to heaviness. Humble yourselves in the sight of the Lord, and he shall lift you up." James 4:8-10[121]

Oh, wait a minute, there's one more story I'd like to tell you, it's really a short one. Do you mind?

This story is about ConnieJean in her pre-school years. The family used to tell it a lot, especially her uncle Seth. It seems at unpredictable times, when family members were busy doing whatever grown-ups do; they would hear this faint, weak voice of a little girl saying at the top of her lungs "2! ...4! ... 6eee!" with what seemed like great pleasure.

When anyone heard the very first number being called out, every adult started running as fast as they could in every direction known to man to reach the location of that faint little voice. Their eyes searched frantically, trying to locate the source of the call that sent chills down the spines of all who heard it. You never heard it twice in a row. There were no second chances to get it right. Seth often retold the story of one visit to the home of Maurice and Mary Helen; on a nice evening they were all out in the yard saying their good-byes, when faintly in the distance they all heard it! "2!" without one word they all started running toward that frail little voice! The men headed for the front and back doors with the women at their heels as they heard "4!"; searching everywhere, high and low, to find ConnieJean. Where is she? Where could she be this time? Then they heard it. "6eee!" as Seth ran through the kitchen door just in time to see ConnieJean flying through the air with a great big grin on her little face, he lurched forward and caught her just before she hit the floor. This had been her highest jump to date; she had never climbed that high before. ConnieJean had jumped from the top of the refrigerator.

ConnieJean never questioned where everyone was before she jumped, she never calculated how far the drop would be, and how long it would take someone to get to her; she just knew she would be caught before hitting the floor, she always was.

Now, that's FAITH!

Grant you, we do not want our little tots jumping from the top step of a stairway or from the top of a refrigerator, but we do want to find the faith and trust of that frail 'little child' who had no fear or thought of not being caught. If only you and I could have faith and trust in the promises of God, our heavenly Father, like she trusted the earthly grown-ups. Just take His word by faith and jump off that ledge of security and fear, take a leap in faith, it's great to fly in God's will and plan, to be unfettered by all our 'self' and earthly fears.

Let go ... "2" ... "4" ... "6eee" ... JUMP! What has God been telling you to do ... "2" ... "4"... "6eee"... **JUMP!!!**

I don't know about you, but this old gal sure could use a break; my voice is getting so raspy and faint I can hardly make out what I'm saying!

Oh, wait a minute! I'll be right back.

No, on second thought come on. Let's go raid the kitchen again. I always like that idea when I need a break! Suppose that's why those old ugly pounds keep sneaking up on me? Oh well, I'll worry about that later. I'm game if you are!

Maybe we should just stay inside; those deck chairs were beginning to get a bit uncomfortable for me. Besides, we can get at those snacks a lot easier inside.

But, before we go in, did you notice that gorgeous bush over there along the fence, isn't it just beautiful! I think the gardener;

- sure, I have a gardener, so do you! It's called "a husband". As I was saying, I think he said it's a multicolored hydrangea bush. I just love it! This is the first year I've ever heard of a multicolored one. This plant makes me wonder a bit about our "miracle family", see how beautiful it is! Think of each one of those huge flower blossoms as a miracle from God, and the bush as this miracle family; see, none of them are exactly the same, yet each is breath-taking in its own right. Do you suppose that blossom decided on its own to be that color, size, and shape? Was it its decision and choice to be different than the others or more blessed, more beautiful? Do you suppose it did something to make itself more beautiful?

I know, you think I'm a tad touched in the head now, right?

The word of God says "...For the invisible things of him from the creation of the world are clearly seen, being understood by the things that are made, even his eternal power and Godhead; so that they are without excuse:" Romans 1:20[122] We can come to understand the invisible things of God by the visible things of His creation. That plant didn't decide to be a beautiful bush, that was all placed in its seed, it didn't decide not to be grass or moss, its Maker did. That bush is just living out the life and existence its Maker planned for it since before it was even planted in that earth. It's beautiful, yes. But, it doesn't have one single thing to do about that or to bring its beauty into existence; its creator did it all. We don't look at that bush and, in awe, think it must be more holy or more perfect than another plant because it's more pleasing to our eye.

You're right, that is obvious! We know that plant can't change the plan for its existence!

So, where am I going with this???

Well, it just seems to me we are so much like that plant, but with one difference, freedom of choice. We have been given the freedom to choose our Maker's plan and purpose for our lives, or we can choose to fight against that plan. If we choose to accept our Maker and His plan and purpose for our lives, then we can be just like one of the billions of plants in this world, fulfilling His plan; living out His blueprint for our existence. They don't have to struggle to become what He has made them to be, they just accept His plan; they just are! But then, neither are they credited for having chosen to be a beautiful bush and not a handful blades of grass. Nothing that bush did of itself caused it be beautiful or to have breath taking colors to attract God's creatures, birds, humming birds, bees, etc., etc.

I see the miracles in the lives of this family, and anyone else, no different than those beautiful breath-taking blossoms; it catches our eye and we are drawn to view the beauty of it more closely, even be in awe of the splendor of it all. But remember, the bush did not create its beauty and deserves no accolades for its existence. And, my dear friend, neither did this family have any hand in the creation of their mighty miracles, nor do they deserve accolades or awe to be showered upon them. They just, and "only", chose the Master's plan.

Okay, that's enough of that; last one in the kitchen gets the scraps!

I think we have about eaten everything except the kitchen sink; hmm, let's see what I can find.

Are you sure you're not hungry, just a little bite of something? I was just joking. Honest, we have plenty around here to eat for quite some time!

Truthfully, neither am I. But I do really need something to drink. We can get a drink and go into the living room, flop down on the sofa or love seat lounges, and kick up the footrests.

I just might have to be careful about getting too comfortable though, I might doze off or something.

So, what tickles your fancy, coffee; pop; milk; raspberry tea? Or, how's a hot chocolate sound?

Good choice, I think hot chocolate sounds just like what the doctor ordered. The warmth might help my voice a bit.

You really are intrigued by this family, aren't you! Yes, on the most part, they were just plain, ordinary people, but they had their bad days too; they weren't saints by any means. Even though Maurice E. and Mary Helen were raised in church-going homes, they weren't little angels - remember the pool hall Maurice had for a while?

Right, I'm sure there were a few people who would have argued with me about Mary Helen not being an angel.

I was wondering, would you mind if we continued talking about them some other day? I can barely talk.

When?

I don't know, about any time you feel like it I guess. Just give me a buzz to make sure I'm going to be home.

Tomorrow?

Wow, didn't know anyone could stand my talking that much! What is tomorrow, anyway? I've lost track of the days this week for some reason. I know I'm not available on Mondays, Tuesdays, and Wednesdays for some time to come.

Thursday?

Well, I think that will be alright, but let me check to see if that wonderful man of mine has any plans, then I'll let you know. Mind if I call you either tonight or in the morning and let you know for sure?

Good, that'll work!

How's that hot chocolate, did I get it chocolaty enough for you? I really like mine with a lot of chocolate in it. This really feels great; a hot chocolate at my fingertips to sip on, my feet up, and the back as far down as it will go, talk about heaven! God surely must have created lounge chairs and sofas, don't you think???

What, you're going to go?

Lady, you take the cake. Can't believe you want to rush home and get your work done for tomorrow, just in case. Okay, promise I'll call as soon as I have a chance to talk with my hubby.

Hey, don't work too hard! You might be too tired to come back tomorrow.

JUST KEEP LOVING
[Check the Fruit]
~ 10 ~

How about that, back again. Hey, what's in the bags? Snacks! You didn't need to bring snacks.

So, where do you want to sit this time, we hit about all the possible choices yesterday except for the beds. Don't think that would be very comfortable at all, besides, I don't want to eat snacks on the beds. Yep, my voice is back strong as ever. I've cleared my day, so we can talk until either my voice gives out again or you holler, ***"Help!"***

Oh wow, you're raring to go. Let's see, where did we end yesterday? Before we pick up where I left off, I want to tell you what I was thinking last night. I was reminded all plants aren't hydrangea bushes, even all really beautiful plants aren't hydrangea bushes. There are many beautiful plants our Lord has given us to please our senses, express His love for us, and try to explain the "invisible'" things with the visible. Well, I was reminded some of the most beautiful plants with the greatest blossoms (miracles) have blemishes and flaws; some can even be harmful, but still they bloom beautifully. For instance, the rose, I just love roses, especially the climbing ones that just spread out and cover a fence or wall with millions of scented roses. Okay, you're right; "millions" is stretching it a bit. The point is, as beautiful as that rose is, and no matter how wonderful it's scent, it still has thorns; it still has all the characteristics of a rose. And it doesn't matter how great the miracle, or how many miracles our Lord blesses us with, we are still human beings with flaws and blemishes. It is so important that we remember we are but mere mortals, it is God who gives the miracles in our lives and it is Him and only Him who should receive any accolades or praise. At our best, we are just allowing the seed (plan and purpose) of God to do its thing; to accomplish what it was created to do.

Oh, what is that scripture? You know the one that tells of God's foreknowledge of us even before we were born. Don't you just hate it when you can't remember a scripture reference or enough of the verse to locate it! You know, when just bits and pieces of it hangs around right there on the tip or your brain, every time you try to focus it floats off somewhere just out of grasp.

Okay, it's Bible break time. I'll never be able to finish this if that verse keeps teasing my brain!

Well, didn't exactly find what I was looking for, but this one is close enough.

"Thus saith the LORD, thy redeemer, and <u>he that formed thee from the womb</u>, I am the LORD that maketh all things; that stretcheth forth the heavens alone; that spreadeth abroad the earth by myself;" Isaiah 44:24[123]

The point I was trying to make here is if our Lord knew us, and before we were even born/conceived, He had a plan for us, then how in the world could we take any credit for any miracles he bestows on our lives? It was part of His plan even before we were born. Granted, we did have to come to the knowledge of Him and accept Him in our lives; we could have thrown a monkey wrench in the whole works by turning our backs on God. But when we turn our lives over to Him and His plan, how can we take credit for His work in and through us? Not one single miracle, blessing, anointing, or fruit produced, is the work of our hands; it's all God's love and compassion! So folks, when we get to thinking we're special just remember, it's 1000 to 0, God wins by a landslide!

Found it! The scripture I wanted. "Before I formed thee in the belly I knew thee..." Jeremiah 1:5[124] This is what the Lord said to Jeremiah. Just think of it, our Lord knew Jeremiah and He knew us *"before we were formed" (conceived)*!

Another thought along these lines comes to mind, that of false "healers" and leaders. Okay, I know, you're wondering how I can get from plants symbolizing miracles to false healers. Just stick with me here and I'll explain. I am reminded of another story Mary Helen would tell from time to time, with a bit of sadness and, what appeared to be, a tinge of guilt. Mary Helen was talking about ConnieJean and how she seemed to always be sick when she was really young, she just caught everything; no mild case of it for her, either. One of the things ConnieJean was very susceptible to was poison ivy. It just seemed she couldn't go anywhere without catching it; in fact, the doctor told them if they were going to drive past a woods or clump of trees out in a field, they should roll up all the car windows. He felt she could get poison ivy if the ivy was within a two mile area of her, and a gentle breeze was blowing her way. ConnieJean would spend a large portion of her summers lying in bed severely covered from head to toe with poison ivy; it seemed to be a yearly routine. As soon as the ivy started sending its spores out into the air, ConnieJean would catch it. One little 'itsy bitsy' ivy blister found before bed one evening would be a head to toe solid mass of seeping, bleeding, blisters by the next day. Unable to stand clothing, she would lay on the downstairs bed with special bedding under her to protect the bed, and only a sheet laid lightly over her. The doctor would come out to the house to administer medicine and shots.

How does Mary Helen's story symbolize false healers and leaders? Because, in many ways false "healers" are just like some plants - poison ivy for instance. False healers and leaders can put on quite a display, deceiving people into believing it is so beautiful, it must be the real thing. We often admire or seek out what appears to be of God due to the beauty of all the proclaimed miracles. We reason, since we are not seeing miracles in our lives or churches, they must really be a man or woman in supreme standing with God. What's that saying? If it quacks like a duck and waddles like a duck, it must be a duck.

But dear folks, everything that quacks (proclaims) and waddles (walks) like a duck (a sincere man or woman of God) is NOT a duck (man or woman "of God")! We must "know" them. "By their fruits ye shall know them. ...every good tree bringeth forth good fruit; but the corrupt tree bringeth forth evil fruit... Therefore by their fruits ye shall know them." Matthew 7:16-20 (ASV)[125]

"Even a child is known by his doings, whether his work be pure, and whether it be right." Proverbs 20:11[126]

Back to the story, Mary Helen loved beautiful flowers and vines, just like her mother did, and all around the fence in the back yard she had many beautiful flowers and vines. Since money was very scarce, her flowers came from her mother, neighbors, friends, all sharing what they had and from walks through the woods. It was beautiful! But, tucked in among all the other plants and vines was a beautiful vine known as poison ivy. She didn't know it was poison ivy, no one had told her. Maybe they just didn't notice it weaving its way in and around the plants. I have two strongly felt suggestions for plants and healers.

1. Understand, not all beautiful plants (men and women) are safe; some cause harm and spiritual death.
2. Really "know" the plant or vine (all are not men and women "of God"), check them out in the plant book (Bible). If it isn't there, leave it alone! Don't let your eye deceive you by its outward beauty.
3. And, one more of my personal warning bells, if they are too "showy" and self-important with "hot house" care requirements (many stipulations or demands for their personal self-care and comforts), beware. Compare their personal "needs" with that of our Lord. What were His requirements and demands to come and preach, teach, and heal the people?

Now, I just know someone is going to say, "She's just way too naïve, these are different times and we have far different customs." What I am saying is not that they should have a stone for their pillow or no bed to lay their head; but if they are truly a man or woman of God doing "His" will, they should have a **humbleness** of spirit and genuine **compassion** for those he/she is there to *"serve"*. Christ's concern was for the people and their needs, not His own personal comfort.

Whoops - I did say back to Mary Helen's story, didn't I? Okay, let's continue. Needless to say, as soon as Mary Helen learned her beautiful vine was making ConnieJean so deathly ill, she had it torn out by the root; digging deep to remove all trace. We all need to be more like Mary Helen when it comes to our beliefs and those we follow, *if we find their fruit is not according to God's holy word, we need to root it out, removing all trace.*

"My son, *forget not my law; but let thine heart keep my commandments*: For length of days, and long life, and peace, shall they add to thee. Let not mercy and truth forsake thee: *bind them about thy neck; write them upon the table of thine heart:* So shalt thou find favour and good understanding in the sight of God and man. Trust in the LORD with all thine heart; and *lean not unto thine own understanding.* In all thy ways acknowledge him, and he shall direct thy paths." Proverbs 3:1-6[127]

Well, that took quite a while; I don't know if I can even remember where we left off last night.

That's right, we were talking about Mary Helen; you sure have a good memory! Let's see, I think we ended with the story about the pool hall, and Mary Helen taking the gambling money back to the wives so they could pay their bills and feed their families. Can you imagine how hard that must have been to do when they were so poor and food was scarce in their own house? When I heard some of these stories, I thought, although not a saint, Mary Helen had the heart of God for the needs and predicaments of others. Mary Helen so reveals our Father's heart of love, even for an immature child who meant well.

Strangely enough, Mary Helen must have been a 'before-her-time super woman'. When it came to nap time, she always had time to stretch a thick blanket out on the floor and lay down between her two 'little menaces', and ever so lightly write with the tip of her finger across their backs, "I love you," or "I love Sonny" or "I love Connie" until they fell asleep. How like our Father, who will forever love us and tell us in oh, so many ways of His love, even when we have royally messed up His plan. As long as we surrender to and accept His love, He will continue to show us in hundreds of ways how very much He loves; even those who have strayed from His path for them, and temporarily gone their own way. Due to our sensitivity, or lack thereof, we may barely hear or feel His loving words and tender touch, but still He writes "I Love You". It is as we surrender to a calm obedience which heightens our awareness, like Sonny and ConnieJean surrendered to slumber's soothing call, we become more and more sensitive to our Lord's words of love and compassion and His oh, so tender loving touch. When fighting the peace and calm of sleep; tossing, turning, and complaining, Sonny and ConnieJean didn't even feel her feather touch or hear her gentle loving words. But they became more and more aware/alert to her cooing words and healing touch, the calmer and deeper they surrendered.

Oh my precious Lord, teach me how to surrender totally and completely. Remove all struggle and turmoil. By your precious Holy Spirit teach me, guide me into that place in you, Lord, where your voice is clear, and your touch undeniable, where your Holy Word speaks loud and clear to my heart, and I rest secure in your purpose and will for my life. Oh, my Lord, just to be one with you in spirit and in truth, leaning not on my own understanding, but resting in your blessed omnipotence.

In the winters, when it was so cold and they couldn't afford to heat the house, Mary Helen would go into the kitchen while her 'innocent little babes' lay sound asleep in their beds, and turn on the oven and open the door; that would provide some heat for her babies. She was careful to pull the blankets across each door so as not to let any heat escape. Pulling a chair up near the oven door, she placed their little shoes on the door to warm them, and draped their clothes over the warming chair. Then, she would take a blanket and place it on the pulled out oven shelf to get good and toasty warm. Once the kitchen was warm and the blanket toasty, she would take the blanket up the stairs to Sonny's room, quickly wrap him as 'snug as a bug in a rug', and carry him down to the warmed kitchen. Warming the blanket again for the second time, she would hurry upstairs to wrap her little blue-eyed, dark-haired, girl tightly in the comforting blanket and carry her down stairs. There, they would be dressed in clothes, which had been oh so lovingly readied for them, and shoes with the heat of love and caring. They were a poor family, very poor; they often didn't have heat for more than one room, or food for the table like others were eating, or lots of gifts and toys scattered all over the house. But they were richer than most kids; they were rich in love. No matter what they did or didn't do, how they acted or didn't act, they were loved! Oh sure, they were punished for being bad, but they were deeply and truly loved. Do you suppose, the high price they paid, all the pain and suffering, the financial burden they might never get out from under, made the kids much more precious to Maurice and Mary Helen? I wonder.

Even when there was no food, and coffee bread became a 'grown-up party' for each meal throughout the day, or times when one orange and heat on a little girls back from the black pot-bellied stove was Christmas, **there was always LOVE!** It didn't matter if they were being 'little menaces' or 'sweet innocent little angels' they were loved. Isn't that a wonderful portrait of our precious heavenly Father! He just loves, and loves, and keeps on loving! I'm reminded of all Mary Helen's body went through to bring these two loved ones into this world, all she suffered while they were growing up and being 'little menaces'; yet, through it all, she just kept on loving.

So like our Lord and Savior. We hear his gentle voice and feel the heat of his love and presence, but we choose to deny Him and say, "That's just my imagination." We see His loving touch all around us and yet 'choose' to believe all that beauty 'just happened'. Sometimes we realize He really exists (or at least we think He does), and we say, "Not now Lord, later, when I'm old". Sometimes we choose to lean onto our own reasoning and refuse to believe he even exists; but He keeps on loving. There are times we even get mad and blame God for all the pain and suffering, all the problems in our world; things we have brought onto ourselves by our reasoning and choices, but He understands our weaknesses and HE KEEPS ON LOVING, patiently waiting.

MARY HELEN'S TRIAL
[Stomach Cancer]
~ 11 ~

There was to be another trial Mary Helen would have to overcome; another health problem that would threaten her very life. She was diagnosed with stomach cancer. All the tests had been run, and it was conclusive. In those days cancer was the closest thing to a death sentence one could get, and stomach cancer held less hope of survival than most of the other forms. She was to have surgery as soon as the arrangements could all be made; there was so much to do, and what about her two little ones. Someone had to be arranged to care for her babies. What if she didn't survive the surgery - Who would care for her babies?

The time came near, and she was told to go to the hospital the day before surgery for more tests so that the doctor would have all the latest results and information he would need for the surgery. New x-rays were taken, and the cancer was still there in her stomach, she needed to have the surgery as soon as possible. Everything was set; tomorrow she would go under the knife in an attempt to save her life.

Mary Helen came home from the hospital that day carrying her two little babies, one on each hip. She sat them down on the sofa side-by-side and told them to stay there - and they did. Now, THAT'S a miracle! Then Mary Helen went upstairs.

No one seemed to recall how long she was upstairs, how long those two 'Dennis the Menaces' sat on that sofa, or what Mary Helen was doing upstairs. Was she crying? Was she afraid? Was she worrying what was going to become of her little babies? Eventually, she descended down the steps. Something seemed a little different about her, so they said, - but what?

The next day she did what she had to do and, once again, Maurice was taking his 'Toots' to the hospital; once again her life was going to hang in the balance while he stood waiting, unable to do anything.

They arrived a little before her appointment time, and the hospital personnel and nurses said they could go ahead and get the paperwork done and start prepping her for surgery. Mary Helen said, "I want the tests run again before my surgery."

The nurses assured her nothing could have changed in that little amount of time, that's why they do the testing the day before surgery, so there can't be any changes. They explained they knew she was understandably afraid, and didn't want to accept the situation, but she does have to have the surgery and they needed to start prepping her.

But Mary Helen insisted she wanted the tests re-ran. Sometimes our sweet, loving Mary Helen could be a little five-foot-four bull dog if she got a bone in her teeth. They'd never get her to drop it until 'she decided' to let go. She invented the word 'determination'.

The doctor came in and said, "Mary Helen, you know I would not make you go through this surgery unless it was absolutely necessary. I don't want to put you through one more thing, but you have to have this surgery." He tried to explain they had already done all the tests they knew to do; she had cancer and she had to have surgery.

But Mary Helen wouldn't budge. She told the doctor, "I am not consenting to any surgery until the tests are re-done". See, told you she could be a little bulldog!

Finally, the doctor gave in to her demands, stating, "When the tests are complete and the results are the same, you '*will*' let them prep you for surgery, **right?**"

Mary Helen agreed.

When the tests were done, and the results viewed, there was **'*no sign of cancer*'**! - Not anywhere in her whole body!

Mary Helen said she went upstairs last night and talked with God. After talking with God, she said it had to be proven to her there was cancer in her body before she would allow any surgery.

OH, how "GREAT is our GOD, and GREATLY to be PRAISED!

Did you catch that? They had to prove '*there was*' cancer, not that there 'wasn't' any cancer. Maybe I'm being a little 'picky' here but there is a difference; a big difference as I see it. She already knew there was no cancer, and it would have to be proven to her that she was wrong, not that she needed them to prove the cancer was gone. Oh, how I long for that 'knowing' kind of faith deep down in my soul, an unshakable faith that has to be proven wrong, not proven right, don't you?

Remember the story in Matthew when the father brought his son to the disciples to be healed, but they could not heal his son, and then he brought him to Jesus? Here, let me read it to you.

"... I brought him to thy disciples, and they could not cure him. And Jesus answered and said, O faithless and perverse generation, how long shall I be with you? how long shall I bear with you? bring him hither to me. ... Then came the disciples to Jesus apart, and said, Why could not we cast it out? And he saith unto them, Because of your little faith: for verily I say unto you, If ye have faith as a grain of mustard seed, ye shall say unto this mountain, Remove hence to yonder place; and it shall remove; and nothing shall be impossible unto you. But this kind goeth not out save by prayer and fasting." Matthew 17:16-17, 19-21 (ASV)[128][129]

Did they find the key to this miracle-working kind of faith? Did they fast and pray? I truthfully can't answer that question for you, I just don't know. They had found something, that's for sure!

Have you noticed something? From the beginning of this recounting of Maurice and Mary Helen's miracles to this point, there has been no 'healer', no one gifted with the anointing and power to heal, no big production with multitudes of people and an atmosphere of faith. On the most part, it appears they were just going about their lives the best way they could, facing each tragedy or hardship the best way they knew how. Where did their faith come from, what caused God to intervene repeatedly in their lives?[130] Could it be all their suffering and God's miracles happened so '*you*' could hear of His wondrous works, so '*you*' could come to believe and reach out to God for your needs? Could it have been for '*you*' to know you do not need anyone else, no great faith healer, no church filled with the presence and power of God; maybe it was all for *YOU* and *me*. What made them so special?

Well, okay. Maybe 'special' isn't the right word here. I really don't think they felt special when all the tragedies, suffering, and pain, came crashing in on them; when one of them seemed to repeatedly be in a fight for their very lives. Do you? Seems to me they may have felt just the opposite. Lord, why are you allowing all these things to happen to me - to us? Why have you turned your back on us, why are you abandoning us, Lord? What have we done, why are you punishing us?

Now I can't honestly tell you what they thought or said in the quiet times when they were alone with God. Did they only seek out God when tragedy hit, or were they always in communication with Him? Did they whine and complain, feel sorry for themselves? I don't know. What I can tell you is that I never had that feeling when they were telling me about these events in their lives. Never once did I get the idea they felt abandoned, neglected, or abused by God. Neither was there the sense they felt special, 'the chosen ones' of God, because of all the times God had intervened. It seemed to me, more like neither the bad nor the glorious was anything unusual. It was like saying, "There was a bad storm last week, but today the sun is out-shining itself and the breeze is just the right temperature; my kind of weather." Do you know what I mean, what I'm trying to say? Like a meteorologist might explain the atmospheric conditions which produced the bad storm, they seemed to have the attitude that sometimes life just produces hardships and tragedies due to our life styles, choices, conditions, or just because they were human beings.

And God's interventions were like saying, "That's just the way God is," i.e., the sun is shining and the breeze feels great today. Although they didn't say it, I had the impression they felt 'that's just life'. It wasn't God's fault for everything that went wrong in their lives, but neither was it a shock when He came to their rescue. That's just the way God is; that's what He does.

You know, to me that's a deep, quiet kind of faith; one that isn't loudly splashing around and crashing against the immovable shoreline; but still, deep, and constant - peaceful. It's not calm and placid one minute and loudly crashing against the rocks and shoreline the next; it's deep, oh, so deep, and calm.

Oh, I want to tell you what happened!

> Last night I was shown a great waterway spreading out as far as my eye could see, and hovering above the waters, I was taken out to view the waters of the deep. They were gently moving, rhythmic, and calm. There was a deep settled peace about them, and yet I knew things existed in its depths that were unreachable by 'human' ability or understanding. There was tremendous power in its depths.

> I was then brought back to view the waters as they approached the shoreline; loud crashing waves and beautiful sprays of water and mist as it hit protruding rock formations. So beautiful to behold, it was displaying its power, loud crashing waves, and sprays of water reaching six…ten feet high as it encountered each obstacle in its path.

But, I was made to know, although it was pleasing to the human eye and gave rise to mounting emotions of awe, it was shallow waters. There was no real depth to these waters; they were driven by winds of emotion.

Once again, I was taken out and shown the still calm waters of the deep, there were no obstructions, there was no display of power and emotion, but my spirit sensed the very depth and power beyond comprehension lying beneath its calm exterior. As the spirit within me began to swell with its breath-taking awesomeness and power, I longed to explore the mysterious depth of the waters below me. There was an almost overpowering fascination and desire for its brooding depth and power, and yet at the same time there was a hesitation, fear of its 'unknown'. Oh, how I longed to explore its depth, to explore its hidden beauties and mysteries; but, would I be able to withstand the unconstrained power that lies within its depths?

I was shown two ways of exploring these waters. First, I saw myself going down into the waters feet first, struggling, flaying and kicking; fighting the water, as I sank deeper and deeper, bubbles escaped as I fought for breath (I did not experience this struggling, I only saw it happening).

Then, it was as though I was back hovering over the waters again and I had never attempted the exploration of its depth. I saw myself, hands stretched out over my head palm-to-palm, as I slipped through the water's depths head first, diving deeper and deeper. There was no sign of struggle or fighting for breath, it was as though I was created to excel in this environment; freely and easily slipping through the mighty waters.

Following this, I had the knowledge the first way I'd been shown was how it is when 'we' are 'trying' to enter and investigate the depths of God on our own; the second was when we totally surrender to the Spirit and relinquish all controls to Him.

There was one last scene. While still in the water, gracefully and effortlessly gliding through its uplifting caress in unfettered freedom, I sensed, felt, a movement down deep in the depth of the waters, like a movement in the very source of this vast depth was shifting, sliding, and with this movement a deep serge or wave began to develop. This serge, or wave, grew in intensity and power moving everything in its path, pushing everything ahead of it. I saw myself riding in the center of this building force as it pushed its way forward and upward; as it mounted higher and higher. There was no struggle or effort on my

> part. This underwater wave then broke through the surface of the waters growing in height, speed, and power; it kept mounting higher and higher, reaching unimaginable heights. There was no loud crashing or great splashing sprays, only a building of a massive tsunami-wall of power mounting higher and higher. This was a tsunami of the Spirit!
>
> Now I was made to know there is a choice: a loud shallow display, a struggling to explore the things of the spirit ourselves, or total surrender and giving all control to our Lord and His precious Holy Spirit, just riding the waves of faith, power, and God's glory.[131]

Oh my Lord, just to have that deep spiritual faith, not to splash around in the spiritual things of God like little children playing by the sea shore. Oh my God, that I might be out in the deep tsunami of your Spirit, riding its wave of power - your power!"

I don't know about you, but I want that deep, calm faith and move of the Spirit in my life! A faith that doesn't have to be 'stirred up' or 'brought to a boil' to see results, but is gently lifted up in power. How about you? Is it possible the 'stirred up' faith is more about feelings and emotions, and the deep calm faith is 'real true faith'? *Just asking* (she says, as her hands, crossing in front of her, grasp her arms and her body sways backward, away from any possible oncoming blows).

"... it is written, Eye hath not seen, nor ear heard, neither have entered into the heart of man, the things which God hath prepared for them that love him. But God hath revealed them unto us by his Spirit: for the Spirit searcheth all things, yea, the deep things of God." 1 Corinthians 2:9-10[132]

Oh, my most precious Father, please guide me, teach me; show me what I have to learn or do, to follow your path into a deep, calm, true, unshakable, faith in You and Your Word. My dearest Father, I ask this in the name of Your most precious son, Jesus Christ. So be it.

It just seems to me that it all boils down to being obedient to God's will for our lives and His Holy Word, which results in *'all things work together for good'*[133] [remember Romans 8:28]. The word 'all' is very important in this scripture; it means there are no 'good' days and 'bad' days, only obedient days and disobedient days. Either we are in the will of God, and 'all things are for good', or I am outside the will of God - disobedient.

We as humans have put the qualifiers of 'good' and 'bad' on the events of our days and lives, and it is by our emotions or feelings we make these determinations; not the good it is doing for us or others, or the ultimate outcome. The thunder and lightning in the storms are as much a creation of God as the soft, gentle rain of spring, or the sunshine. When our God created the heavens and the earth, He gave it the ability to bring sunshine and storms; but, He said 'it is good' when He completed that day's work. It is all in the plan and purpose of our Lord for the 'good' it ultimately brings to the earth and atmosphere; thus, there are no 'good' or 'bad' events in our lives as long as we are in His will - obedient. It is all 'good', because of the ultimate good it brings.

Does that mean we are expected to become all excited when the atmospheric storms are beating against our homes, our shelters? Although it may not be the norm, some of us do. I just love to watch the power and majesty of God in action during a storm, while I am safely tucked away inside my home or a shelter. But don't you see, it's the same thing with the storms of life. If we are in His will, we are safely tucked inside His will and Word during the storms raging all around us and sometimes beating against our bodies (our spiritual home, shelter). If only we could learn the excitement and anticipation of watching His power and majesty play out in our lives, safe and secure in the shelter of His loving hands, contentedly admiring His handiwork.

Now, *THAT'S FAITH*!

Why do we become so fearful? Why do we run hither and yon seeking earthly help and guidance out of our storms of life, when we have the creator of life living right here inside of us? The majestic, all-powerful creator of all that ever was, or is, or is to come, lives inside of you and me. We run to who or what we truly have faith in and trust.

I can just hear you now, "Sure, it's easy for her to say all these things, but harder to live it!" I know! I am a work in progress, but I'm growing daily.

True faith is not impressed or swayed by the atmospheric conditions of our lives, because it's secure inside the shelter of His will, Word, and presence, every second of every minute of every day. When we aren't secured down in the Word of God and His presence; our thinking, feelings, and emotions, get caught up in the storm and beat against our faith, tearing us even further from His protecting hands.

Just one last question, I promise. What are you going to do when all those outside sources the world provides for you to run to, depend on, feel safe in, have gone away or have been taken away from you; what are you, we, going to do then? There is only one sure foundation, Jesus Christ our Lord![134] [135] I think we have definitely found another 'step to a miracle', deep, strong, faith! Are we 'living the Word'?

Shall we add it to our list of possible 'steps to a miracle'?

1. Seek the Lord with all your heart and soul, fear the Lord your God and serve Him in truth with all your heart.
2. It isn't the denomination or the building you attend, it's the God you worship and serve and how you seek Him that matters.
3. Be a genuine neighbor and friend.
4. Be a faithful prayer warrior on the behalf of others.
5. Care and have concern for the needs of others above your own wants and desires.
6. Feed the hungry, give drink to the thirsty, take in the stranger, cloth the naked, and visit the sick and those in prison.
7. Endure hardships, pain, and/or suffering while maintaining your deep heart-love for others and their needs.
8. Set your heart to understanding.
9. Be fully persuaded 'nothing' can separate you from the love of God.
10. Turn your eyes fully upon Jesus - focus on HIM.
11. Examine your heart, thoughts, and life, from the depth of your soul cry out, "Search me, Oh God."
12. Immediately, heed the voice of the Spirit.
13. Have a 'deep' Word based, abiding faith in God.

Great is Our God... and Greatly to Be Praised!

Oh, wow! Just look at that glorious, flaming, orange sunset, brushing the sky in shades of oranges, pinks, and gray-blues; our Lord's exclamation mark at the end of our day saying, "Remember, though the skies grow dark and your path difficult, I AM with you, in you, and I love you beyond human understanding. The sun will rise again and bring joy and light into your world. Just trust me and it shall be so." The approaching darkness of night is just like the tests, trials, and tragedies that come into our lives, but GOD IS THERE, HE WILL bring back the beautiful light of His word and warmth of His Spirit into our lives in the morning. Even as the brightness and beauty of the fading sunset, our spiritual blessings and His signs and wonders drift into our memories past; we must KNOW the Son is even now on His path to us. He NEVER leaves us nor forsakes us! Just as plants and trees need the night hours, so we too 'need' the night of tests and trials to help us grow strong and unwavering.

Oooh my! Our Lord has washed the heavens with the most glorious bright colors! He says as soon as the darkness begins to close in around you, "I am on my way back to you with all my love and gifts, expect me, I am on my way to meet all your needs and fill your heart to overflowing!"

"For the invisible things of him from the creation of the world are clearly seen, being understood by the things that are made, even his eternal power and Godhead; so that they are without excuse:" Romans 1:20[136]

My precious heavenly Father, my heart's desire is that my eyes be opened more every day to see *'the invisible things of You'*, that I might understand all things, even your 'eternal power and Godhead' by those things You have made. Oh, my Lord, that I will not stand before You on that glorious day *'without excuse'*, but will truly know You by Your word and all the things You have made. We are surrounded by all the wonders of God's creation. The ever changing colors of the sky and clouds, plants and trees given to meet our needs, oxygen to sustain our life, herbs and food for our bodies and to fill our eyes with beauty; animals to strengthen our bodies with nourishment and give joy to our existence; water-ways and falls to edify both spirit and soul.

Oh my Lord, just to hear You speaking to us through each and every created thing. To truly 'see' and to become more like You every day. We have made little gods of those 'things' *You* have created. Help us, oh Lord, to see You through all Your glorious creations, to hear You in the lilting songs of the birds and the rush of the waterfalls, to feel Your tenderness and gentleness in the sweet, gentle breezes of summer softly brushing our face. In agony and despair during our struggles and trials of life, we cry out, "Lord, where are You? Why have You forsaken me?" As Jesus wept for Jerusalem, he weeps for you, "Just open your eyes, I'm here! Open My Word, I'm there! I'm all around you just waiting, waiting for you. I did not leave you; you just shut your eyes to my message that's in the sounds you hear, the sights you see, the senses you feel; I'm right here, waiting for you. Open your eyes!"

Hey, try something for me, will you?

Look all around you, noticing a little bird outside your window or over on a bush or limb of a tree. Now shut your eyes. Has it gone? Did it vanish? Is that bird no longer a bird? Will you forever doubt the reality that the bird ever existed in the first place?

Why not? You can't see it. It isn't chirping.

Great is Our God... and Greatly to Be Praised!

What if that bird flew away while your eyes were closed, and when you opened your eyes it was no longer there? Does that mean it never existed? You never heard its song or saw it fly; you must have imagined a bird. Did you decide it was a figment of your imagination and it never really existed in the first place; in fact, there is no such thing as a bird. After all, if you can't see it, hear it, touch it, then it just doesn't exist and never has existed, right?

Okay, let's take this one step further. Suppose you were born blind and have never, ever, seen a bird. Does that mean there is no bird? As far as that goes, there are no trees, no sun, no sky, no flowers, no rain, right? If you're blind, you have never seen any of those things, so that means they can't possibly exist, right!?

No? Why not?

Oh, you're right; you can hear them, so you know they exist. Well, suppose you can't hear them, now you are both blind and deaf, now what? How would you know they exist?

What about that chair over there - Imagine this is the first time you have ever been here in this room, you are blind and deaf, how can you know that chair is sitting there?

Don't know?

I can think of three ways. One way might be if someone took you around and let you feel other things in this room. If we did that, would you associate a chair with other things you were experiencing and believe there is a chair? If you thought there was a slight possibility a chair could be in this room, how would you find it; checking out all the other things in the room, stumbling around in the dark, bumping into objects, skinning your knees, falling? Would that make you 'know' there is a chair?

How could you know, right? If you had never seen, heard, or experienced a chair before, how could you associate a chair with the other things in a living room?

I got it! What if I guided you over to the chair and you could feel it, maybe walk around it, run your hands over it and feel the texture of its fabric and its structure. Would you know now?

Okay, I can buy that. You would know it is something, but you may not know it's a chair; you can't see it and I can't tell you it's a chair because you are blind and deaf.

Well, what if I helped you to realize you could rest in that object, sit down, lay your head back against its strong support, and place your heavy hands on its armrests. You could be at ease and relax, do you think that would convince you it's a chair?

Right, then you'd believe it's a chair if someone had somehow, maybe hand sign language, explained to you what a chair was and what it did.

It's just like that with knowing there's a God. We are all blind and deaf when it comes to the things of the Spirit; we're so caught up in our humanness, we don't see or hear spiritually. Most of us start out either just not thinking whether there is or is not a God, or we don't believe He exists because we've never seen or heard him. We're spiritually blind and deaf.

We may have been exposed to 'religion' in one form or another sometime during our lives, but that didn't 'prove' there was a God. Someone may have taken us by the hand and lead us to a place we could touch and feel 'something', but that didn't prove there was a God, it only proved there was 'something' there, just like the chair.

If I took you by the hand, and lovingly guided you over to the chair, encouraged you to become familiar with what it felt like, and then showed you how to sit down in it and surrender yourself to its strong safe comfort, then you would 'begin' to know there was a chair and this was, indeed, a chair. But, before I could do that, you would have to be willing to let me guide you, and trust me when I sat you down in it. How would you 'know' it would be alright to sit down in this thing? It could break under your weight, right.

That is also the way to discover God. We are blind and deaf to the reality and things of God, trusting only our own thoughts and reasoning; those things we know and can do for ourselves. It's no different than that chair, it could sit right there in that same spot all the days of your life, but if you never trusted anyone to guide you to it and let you experience it, you would never have known it was sitting there. It was just waiting to take the weight off your shoulders and rest your weary hands, to surround you with support and comfort. You would continue to carry all that weight; like anger, hurt, fear, distrust, just because you were afraid to allow yourself to be guided, just because you can't see or hear God. It's true, you may not see Him or hear Him, but *you can 'experience' Him* and know 'He lives'.

Just BELIEVE; that's the key old Dave found, the key Maurice and Mary Helen found, the key that sustained and kept their families even through the hardest of times, and brought them to the foot of the cross where they, too, learned about the God of all gods. It's so simple, but we make it so hard.

Okay, now I have a couple questions for you. Be completely honest with yourself.

1. If I had an envelope in my hands, and said, "I will give you a great gift if you just reach out and accept my envelope", would you believe there was a wonderful gift inside, and accept my gift? Or would you think, "Is she for real? Why would she be giving me a great gift? What have I done for her, or given her? It must be a trick and she wants to make me look foolish."
2. If I held out my closed hand and said, "I have a key for a brand new car of your choice, the maintenance and gas will be paid for five years; there will be no cost to you. It's yours to enjoy, making your life easier for the next five years." Would you reach out, and accept my gift without doubt and concern, or would you walk away and refuse to accept my free gift doubting it's 'for real'?
3. If you were in a crowd, and I was up on the platform and told everyone, "I have some gifts that will make your life easier from the time you accept it and throughout eternity", would you be the first to rush up and get your gift? Would you hold back to see what others did?
4. If, you saw others come up and leave filled with joy and happiness over the gifts they had received from me, would you then come up and fully believe and receive your gift?

The gift is free, but you must believe *'as a little child'*[137] to receive our Father's heavenly gift.

I honestly believe every promise in the Bible is a gift for you and for me, every one! I know we all say that, often. Then why don't we 'see' those gifts manifested in our lives? God is standing there, so to speak, with his hands outstretched, full of all His glorious gifts and provisions, so why don't you and I have them manifesting in our lives? Jesus paid the price with His life, death, and resurrection that 'all' might receive the gifts of God. Why aren't they activated in our lives? Is there something we're missing, something we don't understand, or are we just not 'really believing' from the depth of our heart and soul and reaching out to receive our gifts?

To me, it's mindboggling that this family received so many wondrous gifts, miracles, without even apparently seeking or wrestling them down from heaven; as I heard the stories it felt like they never really did anything special to get them. They just believed. They mention 'talking to God', but that seemed to be all there was to it; then, things just happened, the miracles came.

"And when they were come to the multitude, there came to him a man, kneeling to him, saying, Lord, have mercy on my son: for he is epileptic, and suffereth grievously; for ofttimes he falleth into the fire, and oft-times into the water. And I brought him to thy disciples, and they could not cure him. And Jesus answered and said, O faithless and perverse generation, how long shall I be with you? how long shall I bear with you? bring him hither to me. And Jesus rebuked him; and the demon went out of him: and the boy was cured from that hour. Then came the disciples to Jesus apart, and said, Why could not we cast it out? And he saith unto them, Because of your little faith: for verily I say unto you, If ye have faith as a grain of mustard seed, ye shall say unto this mountain, Remove hence to yonder place; and it shall remove; and nothing shall be impossible unto you. But this kind goeth not out save by prayer and fasting." Matthew 17:14-21 (ASV)[138]

Do you suppose, could they have been people who fasted and prayed? Is it possible they received more from God because they gave more of themselves to God?

Hmm, how about us, are we people who fast and pray - often?

I really can't say if this family prayed or fasted a lot from firsthand knowledge, and they didn't say anything about fasting and prayer, but they may have felt this was a personal thing between them and God either way. Whether they fasted or prayed or not really isn't that important to us, is it? It seems to me, what is important here is that we want to see God working in our lives, and we've been given a 'step' in the word of God for achieving that goal, prayer and fasting.

You know, most of the time when we really want something badly, we will do about anything in our power and ability to get what we want. At least that's how most of us are about material things and anything we feel will make our lives 'better', 'more comfortable', or 'happier'. It may be hard work and take us a long time to achieve everything we imagine for ourselves, but we believe it's worth it if our dreams come true in the end.

What I'd like to know, is how important is it for you to know 'the truth' about God and the things of God? To be partakers of all the gifts he has prepared for those who seek Him out and find Him. Or, would we rather remain blind and deaf, never to know the comfort of that 'chair', of His wondrous presence and power?

The choice is all yours, all mine. We can sit in the dark, afraid of what's out there in the unknown, or we can venture forth. It's all up to us.

HEY, WHAT'D YOU SAY?
[ConnieJean Profoundly Deaf]
～ 12 ～

Let me tell you about another miracle. Actually, this miracle involved several miracles that led up to a whopper of a miracle.

When Sonny (Maurice L.) and ConnieJean became old enough to go to school, the teachers were always talking about what Sonny said or did that day in school. His teacher said there was hardly a day went by she didn't end up out in the hall laughing so hard she cried. Sonny would get so excited with his little hand up, waving in the air so vigorously it shook his whole body when he wanted to say something, but she knew that's exactly the time he would have something to say that would send her out into the hall laughing. She knew better; her instincts told her it would be a 'laugh in the hall' as she watched him wave his little hand in the air so hard he almost fell off his chair.

I remember hearing about a time they were learning the nursery rhyme:

> What Are Little Boys Made Of?
>
> What are little boys made of?
> Frogs and Snails
> And Puppy-Dogs tails
> That's what little boys are made of
>
> What Are Little Girls Made Of?
>
> What are little girls made of?
> Sugar and spice
> And everything nice,
> That's what little girls are made of.[139]

The teacher said Sonny became so upset he was almost in tears. "No, no teacher, that's not true, that's wrong, it's not like that! Sissy and I are the same; we are twins in two batches!"

After calming Sonny down, and assuring him it was just a story, it was out to the hall for her.

From time to time, another teacher, or the principal, would come along and see her standing there in the hall with her back against the wall next to the door of her room, laughing, and tears welding up in her eyes; they'd say, "Okay, what did Sonny say this time!" Then she'd recount his latest comment or deed. She said most mornings while getting ready for work, she'd wonder, "What will Sonny think up today." She said he brought such joy and laughter into their room and learning experience that it was a real pleasure, and she looked forward to going to school and starting another class each day. (Remember, this was a stillborn baby boy who would be a mental vegetable. Have you noticed the joy and happiness he brought into the world of those who knew him? Sonny was a wonderful gift of God to everyone!)

But, on the other hand, ConnieJean (thirteen months younger than Sonny) seemed to provide a big dilemma for her teachers. During one day's time, she would be doing really great one minute, and the next minute or two she didn't seem to have the slightest idea what was going on. She was always a sweet little girl, or so I've been told; but something just wasn't right. By the time ConnieJean passed into the second grade, to the teacher who laughed her way through Sonny's year with her a year earlier, it was clear whatever was wrong with ConnieJean seemed to be there to stay. Her great times and grades were averaged out over her bad times, and she barely passed into the second grade. ConnieJean didn't seem to be dumb or slow, and she wasn't one of those little kids who just didn't listen; in fact, she seemed very alert and attentive. They just had no idea what was wrong with her or how to help her.

Then one day the 'laughing teacher' had an idea! She was going to keep ConnieJean in her mind at all times for the next few days or so, everything she would say or do would be done in an attempt to find out what was wrong with ConnieJean. For the next few days, she would be the teacher's main focus while she interacted with the class and with ConnieJean on a one-to-one basis; she was determined to find out what made the difference between ConnieJean's good times of understanding and times of a total lack of knowing what was going on. She just seemed lost. I was told the teacher had determined she would make sure ConnieJean could always see her face while she was teaching or talking for a while, then she would change her procedure and make sure ConnieJean could not see her face while she was teaching and talking.

Now that's what I call a real dedicated teacher, she was there to teach, to make sure her students learned as much as they could, and she would do anything she could to see to it they had the best chance to do just that - learn. Can you just imagine where all our illiterate high school graduates would be today if they'd had a teacher like the 'laughing teacher'! Instead of tenure and such things, what if their students had to actually advance on their intellectual skills before a teacher could teach the next year. What if they were so dedicated, they searched out the reason 'why' a student wasn't advancing and growing in knowledge, and found the key to further their learning abilities. What if the teachers 'most important' reason for being a teacher, was the students? What a difference it would make in the lives of all those who had teachers who just liked the 'job' and did their time to bring in a pay check, teachers who were more concerned about themselves and their 'teachers rights', than the students' needs. Thank God for the teachers who 'really' care, those who truly put the need of their students before themselves! All teachers affect the future of our country and the world. Some will make it a better place by preparing those students to think and do the 'right thing' for mankind, others will cause the deterioration of our country and world as we know it by producing students who do not think. Students who are not prepared for the world that lays before them . . . students who only know how to 'get by'.

Praise God for dedicated teachers!

Whoops, sorry about that, guess I should get off my little soap box and get on with the story about ConnieJean. It's just that I don't think most of our teachers today realize how important they are to their students' future lives, and to our country and the world around us.

Great is Our God... and Greatly to Be Praised!

Okay, back to ConnieJean's story and miracle. Where were we? Oh, I remember, we were talking about the dedication of her second grade teacher and what she did to try and help ConnieJean.

I can't tell you how many days this continued, or if it was a period of weeks or more; but as I understand it, one day ConnieJean went home with a note for her mother and father from the teacher, principal, and superintendent. To everyone's shock and dismay, it said ConnieJean was no longer to attend classes, as she is profoundly deaf and they were not equipped to teach deaf students.

ConnieJean deaf? - Not their ConnieJean! Maybe she was a little disobedient and ignored you from time to time, but she was not deaf. They would have known, wouldn't they? How could she be deaf and they not know? She can't be deaf; she talks like everyone else her age. How could she have learned to talk if she was deaf and couldn't hear the spoken words? It just can't be true!

Imagine how they all must have felt - her family and friends- hearing she was profoundly deaf and not one of them ever had the slightest idea; it never crossed their minds that little ConnieJean couldn't hear them. Poor little thing, still battling health problems from birth and couldn't seem to put on hardly any weight at all, and now she's deaf, too. Surely, she must have just lost her hearing recently since she can talk. What in the world ever happened that caused her to lose her hearing.

I wasn't told, but can't you just imagine trying different things to test, to prove your little girl can hear; then going to the doctor and hearing those terrible words, "She is profoundly deaf in both ears". "But doctor, how, what happened, she's been just fine. What happened that caused her to go deaf?" Then to hear the doctor say, "ConnieJean has been deaf for a long time, very possibly since birth, we just can't know for sure. Where you and I have eardrums, ConnieJean has solid bone in both ears, there's no way she's been able to hear for a long time, if ever."

"Doctor, she can talk, just like other kids her age."

"Yes, I know," the doctor replied, "I don't know how she learned to talk or how to make the sounds, but ConnieJean has not heard any sound for a long time, if she ever did. I just don't know how she does it" (But we know how, don't we?)

I can just imagine the frustration mingled with unbelief this doctor was feeling. He, too, had never known little ConnieJean couldn't hear, and he had brought her into this world and cared for her ever since that time. They were family friends. Why, why didn't he catch it much earlier; why didn't he know? I'm sure he wrestled with this in his own heart and mind, as did her family and friends, but the only answer was she acted normal; there were no signs, no indications she could not hear. And, as for her being able to talk normally, there was absolutely no explanation; there was no reason he could come up with to explain why or how she could speak normally. There wasn't even hesitation between the time she was spoken to and her response, she just acted normal (Miracle # 1).

An appointment was set with a specialist in Fort Wayne to see if he could help their little girl hear; to see if there was anything he could do for her. When the time of the appointment came, her daddy held her right hand as they walked into the building and down the long, dim hallway leading to the doctor's office. The doctor seemed like a nice man, and was dressed all in white. He took ConnieJean by the hand and, walking over to a low examining cot, asked her to lie down on its cool sheets and covered her up with a bright white sheet. Then he took another bright white cloth and draped it around her neck and head and said, "Now don't move, whatever you do, don't move your head, okay."

ConnieJean laid there so still, not moving a hair. Then the doctor sat down in a chair beside the cot and once again said, "Now, don't move," and placed his left hand along the right side of her face. In his right hand, he held an instrument that was shiny, long, and very narrow, as he brought it up to her face he repeated again another time, "Now don't move sweetheart," and put it into her right nostril.

ConnieJean came to all covered with blood, the white cloth around her neck was soaked in blood, and the doctor's bright white jacket had blood all over it. He spoke in soft, gentle tones telling her what a wonderful little girl she was and what a great job she had done; she hadn't moved one little bit; as he wiped her face with a soft, warm, damp, white cloth which turned red with blood. He would then get a fresh white cloth and wash her face again, and again, until all the blood had been washed away.

Then helping the tiny little girl up off the cot, the doctor turned to Maurice and Mary Helen and said, "I will not do this again to this little girl, I will not put her through this ever again. The radium treatment did not burn away even a slight bit of the bone in her ears, it didn't even phase it. It would be cruel to put her through this again. Your little girl is deaf; there is no cure for her. She will always be profoundly deaf as long as she lives."

Maurice replied, "We didn't know the treatment would be like this, there is no way we would ever put her through this procedure again."

As they shook hands, the doctor said how sorry he was that he could not help their little girl, and Maurice and Mary Helen thanked him for trying.

Devastated, they went home to begin a new life with their 'deaf' daughter. But for ConnieJean, nothing had changed ***except***, she did get a brand new pair of roller skates for being such a good girl at the doctor's office. Life was no different for ConnieJean; life went on just as it had always been.

You know, as I think about this, there was both a bad side and a good side to this outcome. - well, maybe not really a 'good' side, but a better side. At least now they knew ConnieJean wasn't really being willfully disobedient those times she didn't do what they said, she just didn't hear what they said.

I have no idea how much, but time passed and life went on as usual, except ConnieJean wasn't going back to school.

One day, a blind man in the community asked if Maurice would consider taking him to a healing meeting; the man would provide the car and pay all the expenses. He wanted to go see a man who was going to hold some meetings, a man named William 'Billy' Branham.[140] The way the story was told, I got the impression Maurice had never heard of this Billy Branham before, he didn't know anything about him, and it sure wasn't like Maurice to do something like this, remember, he was painfully shy even around family members (Miracle # 2).

The day came, and Maurice and the blind gentleman got in his car and headed out very early, as they had heard it was hard to get a seat; Branham's meetings were said to fill up hours before the service started. When they arrived, there were only a few people trickling into the auditorium, so they went in to get a seat right up front. I believe Maurice said they were in the fourth row from the front, right in front of the pulpit. As Maurice was helping his blind friend get into the seat, and before he was even able to sit down himself, he heard a voice from the platform say, "You're supposed to come up and help, will you help us?" Maurice turned to see who was talking and who he was talking to. Again the man looked right at Maurice and said, "You are supposed to come up and help us; will you help us?" Maurice checked with the blind man to see if he would be alright sitting there by himself for a while, and then he went up on the platform to help out. He said he figured it was just to move some seats or stuff to get ready for the meeting that evening.

Now I don't know the length of time or what all had or had not happened prior to what I am about to tell you, I'm sorry to say I just don't remember. But Maurice was told, "You are to go pick up Brother Branham at his hotel and bring him to the auditorium, and take him to a room in the back where he can wait and meditate."

Maurice was shocked! He didn't even know anything about this man Branham, and now he was asked to go and personally pick him up for the meeting! Can you imagine how shocked he was at hearing this? Maurice was told not to leave Brother Branham's side, to stay with him the whole time, and when it was time, he was to lead Brother Branham out to the platform and take a seat on the platform. Later he could then lead Brother Branham off the platform and take him back to his hotel after the service was done. I can't remember hearing any details, but I am sure Maurice, or the man in charge, saw to the needs of Maurice's blind friend.

Maurice said it didn't take him long to figure out why Brother Branham needed someone to stay with him, to be his constant companion after leaving his hotel room. Brother Branham was so strongly under the anointing, he needed to be led like a child; his heart and mind was not on the things of this earth and time, he was wholly focused on our Lord. Maurice became his companion each time he had to leave the hotel room and come to a service, then took him back again to his hotel. He said they became close during that time, in fact, it became a friendship that lasted until Branham's death (Dec. 18, 1965); corresponding and talking on the phone from time to time (Miracle # 3).

I'll just bet you thought I forgot all about ConnieJean, didn't you?

Honest I didn't, I'm coming to that. During one of the meetings, I believe the last one, but I'm not sure of that, Maurice was sitting on the platform while Brother Branham was speaking. He was preaching on 'believing and receiving' what God has already provided for each of us. As he sat there listening to the sermon, he said it was like a very sudden awakening, "ConnieJean doesn't have to be deaf! She doesn't have to be prayed for by any special person or have hands laid on her. It doesn't matter how far away she is, I am her father and I can take authority and claim her healing for her!" He looked at his watch and noted the time.

Brother Branham mentioned someone, I believe a child, who had serious digestive problems the doctors could not solve, he said that person would become very ill for three days and vomit up horrible looking, smelly stuff. Branham said after the third day, their health would begin to improve and they would be able to slowly gain some weight.

Maurice felt really bad. Here they had come to the meeting so his blind friend could receive his sight. Not only had he not received his sight, but Maurice had spent very little time with him while they were there. As he was apologizing to his new friend on the way home, his friend said, "No, don't apologize, I believe God's will was done".

When he finally arrived back home again, Maurice went into the house where his wife was waiting. She had heard him coming and met him at the door. Mary Helen said, "You won't believe what happened while you were gone! ConnieJean was playing and all of a sudden she could hear; really, she could 'really' hear!" Maurice asked his wife if she knew about what time that happened. Looking a little puzzled at his lack of surprise, she said, "Yes, I looked at my watch, it was (sorry, I can't remember the time I was told)." Maurice than told her what had happened during the meeting, and when he looked at his watch at the meeting, his watch read the exact same time Mary Helen had said ConnieJean began hearing (Miracle # 4).

ConnieJean became deathly ill for three days and Mary Helen was getting very concerned; but Maurice told her about Brother Branham's message, and they decided to just keep a close eye on her and wait for four days. She vomited up stuff that was so horrible looking; I believe they said it had a gut retching odor to it and was dark green in color. She was such a sick little girl. This went on for three days, as Branham had said; on the fourth day, her sickness left and she very slowly began inching on some weight (Miracle # 5).

Now, I'll bet you don't know what I think was the greatest of all these five miracles. **None of them!**

Did you miss the little miracles along the way, a blind man with a car who wanted Maurice to take him to a healing meeting; Maurice agreeing to go to meetings being held by a man he didn't even know; timid, shy Maurice doing what a stranger said 'he was supposed to do'; obedience, obedience, obedience! If just one of those involved would have refused to do what God planned, it is my belief ConnieJean would not have been healed. It is so important we listen and obey the precious Holy Spirit's lead, and walk through those doors he opens before us. Just imagine; the blind man had to ask, Maurice had to accept, the man on the platform had to follow God's leading, and Branham had to preach the right sermon to touch and quicken Maurice's heart to reach out and believe. You tell me, what was the greatest miracle? The greatest miracle of all was the total obedience of all those involved in the chain of events leading to ConnieJean's healing!

An old song comes to mind, "Trust and Obey." Do you remember the chorus?

♪

"Trust and obey,
For there's no other way,
To be happy in Jesus,
But to trust and obey"

♪

Isn't that just the 'nitty gritty' of it, the bottom line; to receive from our Lord all the marvelous blessings and gifts He has waiting for us, we just need to 'really' trust and obey. The last verse is my favorite; it tells us our reward for trusting and obeying our Lord;

♪
"Then in fellowship sweet,
We will sit at His feet,
Or we'll walk by His side in the way;
What He says we will do,
Where He sends we will go,
Never fear, only trust and obey"
♪[141]

Personally, I like to sing 'never fearing', because when we get to that place with our Lord, His perfect love wipes away all fear. The word of God says "There is no fear in love; but perfect love casteth out fear: because fear hath torment. He that feareth is not made perfect in love." 1 John 4:18-19[142] As we trust, as we obey, we sit and walk more and more with our Lord; and, as we sit and walk more with our Lord we grow into His love, that *"perfect love"* that casteth out all fear.

That's where I want to be, how about you? We can only get to this place in our Lord by trusting His word, His precious Holy Spirit, and by obeying. I'll tell you what, I for one am very glad all those involved in the steps to ConnieJean's healing trusted God enough to obey the precious Holy Spirit!

"… Lean not unto thine own understanding …"[143] When the Spirit speaks to your heart, don't reason it out and try to figure out 'why' you are to do what He asked you to do; don't lean to your own understanding. We don't need to 'understand', we just need to 'trust' our Lord and 'obey' His leading. How many souls have not accepted our loving Lord, how many bodies have not been healed, how many needs of the poor have gone unmet, because we reasoned ourselves out of obeying the precious Holy Spirit's lead?

Oh, how my heart cries out, "Oh, Lord, forgive all my sins of disobedience. Most holy Father, don't let one soul be lost, body unhealed, or need go unmet, due to my lack of obedience. Merciful Lord, where I have failed you, Lord, send someone else in my place that their need may be met. Father, don't allow one to pay the price for my lack of obedience. In Jesus precious holy name I ask it."

As I sit here knowing that great and wonderful day of our Lord is coming,[144] when we shall be gathered to be with Him,[145] when all sorrow will be erased and every tear will be wiped away, and where there will be no pain or suffering.[146] Where will all those souls be who were affected by my disobedience? Will I stand before my Lord and hear the names of all those who lost their way, who stumbled and fell by the wayside, who suffered, because of my disobedience? Will their souls cry out, "Why didn't you tell me? Why didn't you pray for me? Why didn't you give me just a morsel of food or a drop of water to sustain me?" Oh my Lord, don't let one be lost or suffering because I didn't obey Your bidding, oh, not one my Lord! Precious Holy Spirit, teach me, guide me, that I might learn to be obedient to my Lord's will in every way."

How, how do we get to that place of obedience? A good starting point might be Proverbs 3:1-6[147] "keep God's laws in your heart, do not forsake mercy and truth, trust in the Lord with 'all' your heart, lean not to thine own understanding, in 'all' your ways acknowledge Him, be not wise in your own eyes, seek wisdom and understanding." This chapter in the Bible is a good summary of how we should live and some of the benefits to obeying these directives. We should read them, read them over, and over again, plant the seed deep in our heart; that we not sin against God in disobedience. Many scriptures emphasize and reemphasize the importance of obeying our Lord's word and voice. But, I believe there are other scriptures we try to skinny around or rapidly whiz by, for instance: "But if ye will not obey the voice of the Lord, but rebel against the commandment of the Lord, then shall the hand of the Lord be against you, as it was against your fathers." 1 Samuel 12:15[148]

One of our biggest and most important tasks as a parent is to teach our children to obey; one of the biggest jobs of the Holy Spirit is to teach 'us' to obey God's word and His voice. Is it possible this is our biggest, hardest, lesson we must learn during our sojourn here on this earth; a lesson it takes a lifetime to learn (If we even get it learned then). It seems our world says 'obey' when it feels right and you have a desire to do so; the Word says "OBEY". Which voice are you, are we, listening to? To which voice have we taught our children to listen?

Well, while we mull that over in our mind and let it sink in really deep, how about a little break? I sure could use one, how about you? I don't know about you, but it seems to me I've been talking forever! My throat is dry and my back is complaining about sitting here for so long. *It's time for a move*!

Oh hey, do you remember the old chorus, "The Move Is On?" At least I think that's what it was called. I think it goes something like:

♪

"The move is on oh Lord the move is on,
The move is on oh Lord the move is on,
For I have heard the rustling in the mulberry bush
And I know, I know, the move is on.
Move on brother, move on sister, This is the moving day.
Move a little closer
where the streams are flowing,
Move on brother, move on."

♪

Hey, we don't sound so bad together, let's sing it again as we 'move on' to the refrigerator and some snacks.

♪

"The move is on oh Lord the move is on,
The move is on oh Lord the move is on,
For I have heard the rustling in the mulberry bush
And I know, I know, the move is on.
Move on brother, move on sister,
This is the moving day. Move a little closer
Where the streams are flowing,
Move on brother, move on."

♪[149]

Just like eating, that song is 'more-ish', the more you sing, the more you want to sing.

Okay, you take the cupboards and I'll ransack the fridge!
*You want to do **what**?*

THE MOVE IS ON
[Mary Helen's Dream]
13

Are you sure? I know going for a walk is better for us than having a snack, but I haven't given you a bite to eat or a refill on your drink for some time. Are you sure, you don't want something to eat?

You're right. We do eat a lot out of habit or out of boredom. Just look at me and the majority of people we come into contact with every day, we are all over weight. One of the important things about all this weight is, I believe, each bite we take that's not an ingredient the body needs to do its work properly could be one more minute, hour, or day off our lives. I'm reminded of the scriptures that say "Know ye not that ye are the temple of God, and that the Spirit of God dwelleth in you? If any man defile the temple of God, him shall God destroy; for the temple of God is holy, which temple ye are." 1 Corinthians 3:16-17[150] and "What? Know ye not that your body is the temple of the Holy Ghost which is in you, which ye have of God, and ye are not your own?" 1 Corinthians 6:19[151]

From time to time, my mind keeps coming back to a nagging question, have our snacks and drinks become an idol to us? What is an idol? Well, let's check that out before we go for our walk. Do you mind?

Good. The books we want are on the shelf over there in the far corner of the bookcase, about three shelves down from the top.

Okay, here's Easton's Illustrated Dictionary[152], it describes an idol as nothingness, vanity; a thing of naught, a word of contempt; terror (hideous form of idols), a fright or horror; shame, shameful thing (obscenity); word of contempt, dung, refuse; filth, impurity'; likeness, a carved image; a shadow; similitude (copy); a figure, to fashion; a form, shape; a statue, memorial stone; sun-images; device, image of stone, chambers of imagery; a graven or carved image; a molten image; images.

Wow! I would have expected something like likeness, a carved image or a graven or carved image, but not all the rest of them.

Well, would it be possible for our 'over eating' to be an idol? What do you think?

I suppose one look at all this blubber could cause a fright or horror, and you know it is a shame, shameful thing, to let ourselves, myself, get so out of shape.

Okay, you win, let's go on that walk!

Isn't it crazy, we keep saying we shouldn't have it even while we are in the act of lifting our arm to put that next bite of junk food into our mouth? Seriously though, what is the hold over us that keep us from 'doing that which is right'? Are we being deceived by the evil one, being told (like Eve) " . . . Ye shall not surely die"?[153] James tells us, "Therefore to him that knoweth to do good, and doeth it not, to him it is sin." James 4:17[154] To know to do good and do it not *is sin*! If we are indeed the temples of God, and we know certain things are not beneficial to our bodies, some even harmful, isn't it then a good thing to not eat or drink it? Is it not then a sin if we do eat and drink it?

Hey, slow down a bit, I can't walk 'that' fast. You did say 'walk', right?

No, I'm not kidding; can't get my breath, my legs are so weak. I've got to stop.

Okay, just let me catch my breath, and then we can sit down on that bench over there. Go ahead; I'll be there in a minute.

Sure, I'll be alright; be there in a minute.

This is better.

What do you think now, is eating all that junk food a sin? Look what's happened to me, I can't even walk a couple blocks without coming apart at the seams. This is just no way to treat the temple of the precious Holy Spirit of God. It's time to do something about it, starting now; more walks and *healthy* snacks! How can I be of any service to my Lord when I can't even catch my breath?! Let's see, how did that verse go?

Right, you've got it, "Therefore to him that knoweth to do good, and doeth it not, to him it is sin." James 4:17[155]

Okay, I think we can go on a little more. Is there another bench down the way?

Oh no, I don't want to go back home yet! Quitting will not help me get any better. You know it's just like serving our Lord, we just can't quit when things get a little rough; we have to press on to the 'higher plane'. Just stop momentarily when we have to, catch our breath, and press onward. You know, I think there's a chorus about a higher plane, isn't there?

How does it go? Something like, 'plant my feet on higher ground?' Doesn't that just irritate you when something is buzzing around in your head and you just can't seem to grasp it? It sure does me. Maybe that's called 'old age', ya think? If I was home, I'd just dig out an old song book and look it up.

Right! That sounds like it.

♪

"Lord, lift me up,
And let me stand,
On heaven's table land,
A higher plane,
Th an I have found;
Lord, plant my feet on higher ground"

♪

… Seems to me we're missing something. Doesn't it have something in the chorus like "by faith on heavens" something or other?

That's it! I believe you've got it!

♪

"Lord lift me up,
And help me stand,
By faith, on heaven's table land.
A higher plane,
Th an I have known,
Lord plant my feet on higher ground"

♪156

By Jove, I think you've got it! If we'd only open our eyes, we'd see that is what life is about, every trial and hardship, it's just trying to lift us up to a higher plane of growth and understanding. Isn't God something! It's like this is the growing and proving ground, once our product is tried and tested, it is then moved to the showcase, the higher ground, Heaven!

Just think, one day we'll stand before our creator, the one who imagined us and created us, brought us into being. What a glorious day that will be!

Oh wow, I do believe we just ran smack dab into another song.

♪

"What a day that will be,
When my Jesus I shall see,
When I look upon His face,
The one who saved me by His grace,
When He takes me by the hand
And leads me to the promise land.
What a day, glorious day that will be."

♪

One more time!

♪

"What a day that will be,
When my Jesus I shall see,
When I look upon His face,
The one who saved me by His grace,
When He takes me by the hand
And leads me to the promise land.
What a day, glorious day that will be."

♪157

I don't know about you, but this ole lady is about to have a camp meeting! What a God we serve!!!

♪

What a mighty God we serve,
What a mighty God we serve;

> Angels bow before Him,
> Heaven and Earth adore Him,
> What a mighty God we serve
> ♪158

Glory … GLORY … *GLORY!* **PRAISE the LORD!**

What did you say?

Oh right, they did look at us sort of funny. Suppose they think we're crazy or something?

"Good afternoon. What a beautiful day the Lord has given! I pray it's blessing your soul like it is ours."

Lord, bless them and bring them to the knowledge of your saving, healing, loving, presence. Amen.

Who needs all that junk food, when we can feast on the sweet manna from heaven! Bring on the milk and honey; I believe I've just felt a glimmer of heaven in my soul!

Now that we're headed back in the direction of home, I'm reminded of one of the Mary Helen incidents they told me about. Would you like to hear it, if I can walk and talk at the same time that is?

Well, it does take a touch of skill to do both feats at the same time, the mouth is moving up and down while the feet are moving forward and back. It's sort of like that 'rub your belly and pat your head' thing, or is it 'rub your head and pat your belly'? Oh well, you get the idea. Then, to make matters worse, add to the mix breathing.

Oh no, I'm alright, just trying to be funny, I guess.

Back to Mary Helen and 'moving on', if you can listen and walk at the same time, that is. For some reason I seem to think you have the easiest part of this arrangement!

Great is Our God... and Greatly to Be Praised!

This incident popped into my mind while we were singing, "The Move is On." I was told Mary Helen had a few dreams in the past that came true; one was about a little baby who was on its way into this world, but she was shown in the dream the baby would not live, and the health problem that would cause its death. How hard that must have been to know your first little nephew, who was yet to be known he was even on his way, would not live. They really did not go into any details as to what she said or did because of the dream, or if she said or did anything but wait and pray, but they did say everything happened just as it had in the dream.

But on the brighter side, one day Mary Helen woke up and told Maurice she would like to go for a ride; she'd had a dream. Maurice knew by this time when Mary Helen said, "I had a dream," she was talking about one of her 'special' dreams. So they got around and went out to the car. When he ask where she was wanting to go, she said she didn't know where it was for sure, but she knew how to get there; so she proceeded to direct Maurice which direction to head out from the house, and when to turn right or left, according to her dream. She recalled all the sights and sounds along the way to their destination. They pulled away from the curb in front of their little home on Monroe Street, driving north to East South Street, and following the State Road 101 signs, they made a right on Main Street and continued across the railroad tracks and out of town. What a pleasant drive as they proceeded through Townley and Woodburn where State Road 101 now headed straight north.

As I remember, it was a very pleasant day and they were fully enjoying the ride through the countryside. Mary Helen very well may have seen the cattle grazing on the little hills and valleys and said, "My Father owns the cattle on a thousand hills," as she so often did throughout her life.

Now crossing into DeKalb county, they continued north through Butler, into Steuben County, and on to Hamilton Lake. At the crossroads of State Roads 101 and 427, Mary Helen said, "This is it! Stay on this road," pointing down East Bellefontaine road. You could hear the excitement in Mary Helen's voice, "It's just a little ways down this road, slow down, Maurice, slow down!" They came to a small open field on the right, and Mary Helen said, "That's it, that's the house! Pull over."

As they sat on the side of the road, across the street from 'the house', she told Maurice all about her dream and that, "Th is is our house, God said we were moving here." Almost teary, she talked about the big house on the hill, the barn and chicken coop out back, and, "Did you see the little house sitting behind the main house when we came by? Oh Maurice, God is going to give us this house."

Maurice knew her 'special' dreams always came true, but he just could not see how this one could. They were so in debt with all the medical bills and they had no savings; there was no way they could afford to move, especially to a house and land like this. He smiled and said, "Toots, it isn't for sale. There's no for sale sign in the yard anywhere."

"Oh, that's okay, just drive around the circle drive and stop near their back door."

"You just can't go up to the door and tell them they have to move because God said He's giving you the house," Maurice said with a twinkle in his eye. "We'll just drive up here from time to time until it goes up for sale. Maybe by then we can afford to buy a house."

"We can just go up to the door and introduce ourselves, tell them we are interested in buying their house, come on, what would it hurt," Mary Helen said with a pleading determination in her voice.

"Are you serious?" he replied praying she wasn't 'really' serious.

"Just pull into the lower drive and circle up around the back of the garage so we can see more of it, and stop by the walk to the back door. You don't have to go with me if you'd rather stay in the car."

Maurice was feeling all the tightness and discomfort that comes when his shyness kicked in, as he pulled into the lower drive and very slowly drove around the circle drive; with Mary Helen pointing out all the wonderful things she saw. "Are you sure, we could just keep going, if anyone sees us they will think we pulled into the wrong driveway or something."

With her hand already on the door handle, she said, "No, just stop right up there; it'll only take me a minute to introduce myself."

So, to make this long story shorter, suffice it to say, Mary Helen went up to the door and talked to the old gentleman of the house and they were invited in for coffee and a snack. If you knew Mary Helen, you'd know that was a given, people loved her from the first 'hello'; and yes, Maurice did manage to leave the car and become comfortable with this dear sweet elderly couple.

After a real nice visit, the couple told them they really had no plans to sell the property, they were so sorry, but they sure did enjoy the visit and to come back again anytime. Mary Helen was already prepared with their name, address, and phone number written on a note card; handing them the card she said, "Here's our phone number if you should ever change your mind," as they were walking out the door.

One week later Maurice and Mary Helen received a phone call; the couple had driven to Angola, saw a house they liked, and bought it; the Hamilton Lake property was theirs if they still wanted it. The price? "Well," they were told, "we will get together and see what you can afford, and then you can just pay us as you have the money to do so; we don't need it right now."

Okay, you tell me, does God do what He says He will do; even the impossible? What a wondrous God we serve! You see, it really is true, our God can do anything, even the unimaginable!

Right, it's unbelievable. That's what they said. They'd agree on a price, and they could pay as they could afford to do so. How many homes have you bought with a friendly visit, a handshake, and a dream?

Me either!

But, if God did it for even one person, we have the right to believe He can do it for us too, *if* we are truly serving Him and He feels we need it. Can you imagine what it must have felt like the day they moved into the home God gave them! Our God really, truly, is a great and wonderful God who loves His children and takes care of them; *if,* they let Him do so by being obedient. He won't force Himself on us, not even His care and kindness. How is it 'anyone' would not want to serve a heavenly Father who is so loving and so generous to His children? I just can't wrap my mind around it, why anyone would not choose to accept and live for our Lord?

After walking in silence for a while, thinking on the greatness of our heavenly Father and the denial of so many people to accept Him, I spied another bench just up ahead and said, "Do you mind if we take a little breather sitting on that bench up there?"

Oh, this is nice. Just enough sun speckling through the leaves of this big ole oak behind us, and the kiss of that ever so gentle breeze; doesn't it feel like your face is being gently caressed by our master Maker, He is saying, "I love you and will take care of you my child." Our Lord and Maker has created so many ways to show us, tell us, of His love for us, but sometimes we get too busy with our earthly lives and endeavors to slow down and shut our eyes, to just listen to His wonderful tenderness and love for us. On a day like this, I really love to take some time and sit with my eyes closed, enjoying His gifts to us and listening for His still, small voice, communing with our Holy Father spirit to Spirit. Times like this always makes me think of that song:

♪

I come to the garden alone,
While the dew is still on the roses,
And the voice I hear, falling on my ear,
The Son of God discloses.
And He walks with me and He talks with me,
And He tells me I am His own,
And the joy we share as we tarry there,
None other has ever known.

♪159

You know, that song is sung at a lot of funerals, but it's not a song of dying to me, but of coming to that secret place we share with our Lord, and Him only; coming into that garden, that secret closet of our heart, and feasting on His holy presence and word. Have you ever had the experience of knowing someone was watching you or standing near you but not seeing them, then turn around to see them standing within a few feet of you? That is how it feels when my Lord meets me in our secret garden. His presence is so strong, and so real, it feels as though if I turn around He will be standing there in plain view. His presence is so real and so strong there is no denying it - He is there! You just can't see Him.

I know, you are probably thinking, "Oh, it's her imagination," right? Well, try something for me, okay?

Have your spouse or loved one leave the room, then go into the middle of the room, shut your eyes and just stand there. You don't have any creaking floor boards, do you? Okay, then, at an undetermined time, have that stocking-clad spouse or loved one enter the room, silently coming closer, and closer. Without hearing them, when do you know they are there, near you? Tell me, can you feel their presence?

My father could be seen ever so quietly slipping up behind mother as she was lost in her cooking. When he would see you coming into the room, he'd put his right index finger up to his mouth and his lips would form the shape they made when he would go 'shhhh'. She would be so lost in her work, she wouldn't hear him or sense his nearness. He would ever so gently slip his arms around her, drawing her back into his chest and whisper something in her ear. Relaxing back in his arms, letting all the tension and stress of her work just drain away, the most peaceful, beautiful smile would slowly spread across her face.

Well, that's the way it is with our Lord. I know He's there because I can sense, feel, His presence right there in the room with me. All God's children who spend enough time with Him in prayer and reading His word can come to the place they experience His presence; you will have found the 'secret garden' of your heart where God dwells. His gentle, loving arms will slip around you, giving you strength and peace from the stress and labors of the day. The sad thing is, God dwells there all the time, just one prayer away, but He often goes unnoticed. We reject Him. We deny His existence. But He waits; He loves.

It just breaks my heart as I watch so many wonderful people, really nice people, miss out on knowing the true and living God. Who brought all things into existence; our Lord, who meets our needs and heals our bodies; our Lord who can raise the dead; protect from the instruments of war; heal cancer and profound deafness; and our Lord who can guide and direct us.

Saying there is no God because you can't see him, is much like shutting your eyes and saying there are no trees, flowers, or green grass, because you can't see them. Saying it's impossible to sense or feel the presence of an almighty God is like saying you can't feel the breeze brush across your cheeks; they can't be seen, but they both can be felt. Just as the trees and flowers are real whether I am blind or my eyes are closed, so it is that God is real, even though we are blinded to the truth of His existence or have willfully closed our eyes.

Seeing is not the test for reality. If it were, there would be no reality of any kind for the blind.

I once knew a man, blind from birth, Tommy, who could run across fields and jump fences and creeks without stumbling or falling and without running into anything. His inner sense of 'feeling' the existence of things was honed to a fine degree. He would take off running, and if anything was put in his path he would sense it and run around it.

It is with this inner sense we can come to God in a very real way. He is there; you just have to find him.

ON A QUEST
[Elton's Questions]
~ 14 ~

Okay, for example, let me tell you about a 'sensing' which led Maurice to find answers to some very serious questions his brother had about life and death, especially death.

Maurice's older brother was in the hospital in Fort Wayne, and in serious condition (let's see, I started first grade when I was seven and moved to our 'new house' the year I started the fourth grade, so this had to be sometime between 1952 and 1955). If my memory serves me right, he had a bad heart attack, but when they started running tests, it seems there were other things wrong with him, too. He was worried. He knew he wasn't prepared to die, so during one visit he began to ask Maurice some questions about life and death; about life after death. Maurice wrote down the questions, and said he would see if he could find the answers for him; he did not know the answers to his questions either. Maurice had studied and prayed, but had not found the answers he so desperately wanted to be able to give his brother.

Since they were now living in Hamilton Lake, Maurice got up early the following Sunday morning and told Mary

Helen he was going into Fort Wayne to see his brother, but he wanted to go to church first and try to talk with a minister after the service; he wanted to try and get the answers to his brother's questions. After eating a little breakfast, Maurice headed into Fort Wayne seeking answers to questions that now haunted him. He really felt he had to get the answers to his brother as soon as he could, since they didn't know what was going to happen. When he arrived in Fort Wayne, he realized he didn't know any of the churches in town and had no idea where he should go, so he just started driving around thinking he would just pick out a nice looking church on his way to the hospital. When he pulled in front of the first church of his choice, thinking he would park and attend their service, Maurice experienced a sudden coldness that came over him and he said he just couldn't go into that church; so he drove on. As you may know there are a lot of churches in Fort Wayne, so he had a lot to choose from as he drove. I remember Maurice saying that same experience happened two or three times, and he was about to give up on finding a church. Services would be starting soon, and he didn't want to walk into a strange church late and draw any attention to himself.

Looking at his watch, he decided he'd try a little church up ahead and then give up if that same thing happened again. As he approached the church, he was wondering if he would feel that same coldness again, so cold he just could not have sat through a service like that.

But now, as he was pulling up in front of the little one floor church on Winter Street, he began sensing a new feeling; a warm, comfortable feeling came over him as he sat there in his car. Well, this would just have to be the church, he had no time to look for another one and still be able to go in before the service started. In fact, the singing was already starting as he walked in and, after a couple friendly handshakes; he took a seat in one of the back pews.

These people really liked to sing! They were singing with all their hearts, and raising their hands. They looked so happy, but why were they raising their hands, he wondered. It didn't take Maurice long to figure out these people were worshiping God in a way he'd never seen before; they really seemed to mean it from down deep in their hearts and souls.

I can't remember hearing him say if he ever felt at ease enough to join in the singing, or if he just sat there observing this new, strange way of worshiping and singing in church. As the service came to the time the minister was going to deliver his sermon, he stood a few minutes behind the pulpit. Then, raising his eyes and looking out over the congregation he said, "I can't preach the message I have prepared for this morning's sermon. As I sat there during the song service the Lord gave me some questions I am to answer; just answer a few questions."

Of course Maurice's ears picked up as he intently wondered what was going on, he had never heard a minister get up and change his sermon right before he began preaching; either it had not happened before or those ministers just didn't tell anyone. This church, this service, sure was proving to be a different kind of church!

After a short time of explaining, the pastor began to read the questions one by one, giving the answers to each question; fully explaining the answers he was giving with many scriptures to support his explanations.

Maurice quickly pulled his little piece of paper out of his pocket as the first question was read. It sounded familiar. Shocked, he sat there, pen in hand, taking notes and writing scripture references as the minister appeared to read the questions right off of his little piece of paper, word for word. Not only did the pastor answer his questions, stating them word for word, but he did them in the exact same order as they had been written on his own paper; just as Elton had asked them!

By His very presence, our Lord had guided Maurice to the right church where the answers to his questions would be obediently received and given. What a wonderful heavenly Father and God! One who even cares about the questions we ask, and provides the answers we need.[160]

Maurice had found a church who knew how to worship God in a way he had never seen, a church who knew how to listen and obey when God spoke. This was for sure a different kind of religion! And it 'felt' good, everyone was so happy and friendly! Although he didn't know even one of them, they all shook his hand and talked with him as if he were an old friend who had just returned from a lengthy trip.

Maurice was almost reluctant to leave, but he had to get up to the hospital to see Elton; answer his questions, and tell him all about 'how' he got the answers.

That, my dear friend, changed the lives of Maurice and his family forever. He had to bring his little family to this church so they could experience the love and genuine caring these people had for one another, and yes, even for strangers, too.

Great is Our God... and Greatly to Be Praised!

The very next Sunday, the four of them walked into the church and up to one of the pews about halfway back from the pulpit, sitting on the right side of the church. But, it wasn't long until they found their way up to the front (about four rows back from the front) and in the center section of the church, they didn't want to miss a thing!

I can't tell you how many services they attended, maybe one or two, I don't know, until they were finding themselves at those church doors every time they opened. In fact, they were one of the first to arrive for many of the services. And, the forty mile (one way) drive was filled with singing and excitement about the service they were either on their way to attend, or the service they had just left. It was great! In the summer, to save a little money (more gas money to go to church), Mary Helen would pack bologna sandwiches, a bag of chips, sliced cheese, and when they could afford it, each one could have a small bottle of pop. They would go to a park and have their lunch, then take a nap in the car until it was time to go back for Sunday night's service. It was like going on a small vacation every weekend!

They just couldn't wait to go back to church again[161], to sit in the very presence of God, and sing; *oh, what beautiful singing*! Everyone happy and smiling, and they all had a squeaky clean shine on their faces; they all seemed to just beam – radiate - the love of God.

It was great!

A NEW BEGINNING
[ConnieJean Remembers]
~ 15 ~

Their very first Easter came and they were eager to get to the church. Since they had started sitting in the front center section, ConnieJean would tend to lose her concentration on the service, especially during the song services, and become focused on the people sitting in the very front of the right section; there was a lady sitting in a chair in front of the pews, facing the pews. It was so fascinating. The lady appeared to be sitting there talking with her hands as the leaders prayed, talked, during special songs by the choir or individuals, for the song service when the congregation was singing, and even for the preaching and altar call. Her hands flowed as if dancing in air with every word or note. And her body, her body seemed to be expressing what her hands were saying like fluctuations of tone and volume of our voices. It was all there - joy, anger, and everything in between - all in her hands and body.

The people sitting in the first few rows saw everything we heard! It was so fascinating, so mind-boggling, without voice and words they were able to receive and understand everything through their eyes! What a wonder, what a gift! The deaf could hear without hearing one single sound. During the song service, they would 'sing' with their hands right along with us as we sang praises to our Lord and Savior. It was so fascinating to ConnieJean. It was so beautiful, a language of grace and rhythm; it was hand dancing, flowing art. Art that somehow flowed right into ConnieJean's very being.

This Easter Sunday was going to be different, special; Sonny and ConnieJean were going to experience something even more wonderful than watching the lady's dancing hands. I cannot tell you what the pastor preached on that morning, nor can I tell you what was said in the alter call, but what I can tell you is something was happening deep down inside ConnieJean. Something she didn't understand, something so strong it could not be denied; a 'need', a 'drawing'. There was no memory of 'fighting' the deep feeling, only its growing intensity as she sat there. It seemed she would literally burst open from its engorging. When ConnieJean saw Sonny get up out of his seat, without question she jumped up out of her seat and followed him to the altar in front of the right-hand pews where they knelt, side-by-side. ConnieJean stated, "All I truly remember thinking was if this is good for Sonny, then I want it too!" It was then this growing seed of intensity within her burst into a glorious blossom of peace and joy, the heaviness of life just lifted off of her and she felt as though she was light as a feather; such unexplainable lightness and joy. She just couldn't explain it. There had been good times, happy times, times of laughter and carefree play; but those times were nothing compared to what she felt this day. Something was totally new and different in her and about her now! Jesus had come into her heart, and there was a mental, emotional, and physical, difference in ConnieJean when she rose up from that blessed altar that day. She was a totally new person in Christ Jesus!

There were so many changes!

Let me explain. I suppose the first change anyone noticed was that I wasn't that same sad little girl. It was said many of our family and friends questioned our new found 'religion', until they saw the change in ConnieJean. I didn't stop and think, "Oh, now I have to think and act this way or that"; there was an immediate change in my character and personality. On that April 5, 1953, Easter morning, I became a new creature in Christ.[162] At the age of eleven, I was filled with the joy of the Lord. The change in me was so noticeable, other classmates came and wanted to know what made me different. One classmate came in the classroom where I was eating my sack lunch, I don't know what was said by her or to her, but both girls knelt beside ConnieJean's little school desk and my little friend gave her heart to Christ.[163]

I was so happy and life seemed so good!

A couple weeks later, mother and I stood in the row behind the first pew at church. We had moved up from our regular forth row service seats to the front row for the altar service. Oh, what a service; the altars were full and there was no room anywhere around them, especially the center section altar. It was like heaven or something, standing there watching, listening, and finally putting my hands up like the others were and standing there crying tears of joy; oh, so happy.

Something strange happened; when I opened my eyes I was no longer standing in the first row of the center section,

I was sitting on the center section altar, speaking in a strange language. I couldn't seem to stop, nor did I really want to. I didn't understand what was happening, but it sure made me feel happy, joyous; filled with the love of my new friend and Savior. There were no words in my language to express my joy and love for Him; but He seemed to like this new language I was speaking, it felt as though He was pleased with it.

Mom, or 'me-mom' as I called her, said I had started to dance, and danced all through the rows and isles without touching anything or anybody. She said our pastor told the people around where I was dancing, "She's full of the Holy Spirit, sit her down and she'll start speaking in tongues," but no one wanted to stop me from dancing. She said it so blessed; everyone was watching me dance in the Spirit. At one point, I danced up by where pastor was on his knees praying with some men at the altar, and he gently sat me down on the altar. Mom said such a beautiful heavenly language just flowed out of me as I sat there worshipping my Lord and my Savior.

About two weeks later, when I was baptized in water, I came up out of that water full of the Holy Spirit and speaking in tongues; lost in the Spirit. I'm told I was helped out of the baptismal and sat back out of the way where I continued worshipping in the Spirit, while they continued baptizing other new believers in water. Once again, my brother and I took a deeper walk together in water baptism in obedience to our Lord's instructions in His holy Word.

My life had changed again. Oh, how I loved to talk with my Lord and feel His presence in me, around me; He was everywhere! His presence and love filled every waking hour. You know, after all these years, He is still just as real, just as precious, as He was way back then. He fills my heart and life with His precious presence and love every day.

OH, *GREAT IS 'MY' GOD, and GREATLY TO BE PRAISED!*

Sonny and I had a new past time now; we would go up in the barn hayloft and arrange the bales of hay and straw around like pews in a church. Sonny would stand a bale on end for his pulpit and ConnieJean would sign to any dolls or animals that would stay still long enough to be their church members. Occasionally, well, often, I would have to jump up and 'catch' one of our 'pew sitters' (usually one of the cats or bunnies), and sit them back down in their proper pew, which was a little upsetting to the preacher. But we would all get back in our places and the service would continue. Eventually, one or two of our congregation would curl up and go to sleep and the others would wonder off, but there was always the captive audience of the dolls and ConnieJean.

These were such wonderful days!

Oh, I know I'm just rattling on and on, but I can almost relive those days when I think about them; feel the joy, feel God's presence. It was just great!

It was so beautiful at night lying in my bed upstairs; dad could hum and whistle a couple harmonizing notes all at the same time, but he wouldn't do it until he thought everyone was sound asleep. Then, when 'me-mom' had fallen asleep from the exhaustion of a long hard day, and Sonny was making 'sleeping sounds' in his room, the notes began drifting up the stairwell and through the floor vents into my room; like the tune of a pied piper. I followed every note as he made music to his Maker. I just couldn't understand how he could make it sound like three, sometimes four, people were down there humming and whistling. Some of my fondest memories are lying next to Lady, our Golden Sable dog, and falling off to sleep surrounded by the Holy Spirit's presence and the heavenly sounds of my father whistling; warbling.

Have you noticed something?
Like what?
Well, have you noticed that *my references to ConnieJean have changed*? Hmm, guess my references to Maurice, Mary Helen, and Sonny have changed too. *Did you catch that?*

At the age of eleven (before she became a Christian), ConnieJean had almost NO memories, she could not recall anything about her earlier years except those things 'others' told her had happened. She lived in the 'here 'n now', each day was a new beginning. In later years, I wondered if my lack of memory was maybe due to being so ill all those years, maybe my mind just blanked out all the weakness, sickness, pain, and struggle. Maybe it was because I had been deaf and didn't hear and see all the things that had happened. I reasoned, if a person doesn't hear a sound or word, they may not turn to see what was happening; but then I wondered why I didn't even recall times and events that would indicate something was missing.

There was one incident, but only one I recall. There was a time I could see myself out on the playground on the merry-goround, then suddenly everyone else turned to look towards the school, and some even started running toward the building; but then they all went back to playing. At first, my thought was, "It's time to go back to class", but then they all came back out to the playground. I never did figure out what had happened that day.

I can't remember there being any 'sound' in my life, but neither were there memories of there 'not' being any sound; interestingly, neither was there any sound in my early dreams as far as I know.

Like being deaf, I appeared 'normal', maybe a little on the slow side of normal, but no one realized I had very little, to no, memory. I seemed normal enough I guess. It was just like being able to talk normally even when I couldn't hear; there were just no memories of those early days, no earthly memories.

Jesus changed it all! He made me whole and normal! My first day with my Lord, the day I was 'born again' and received Christ into my heart and life, was truly the first day of my life! It wasn't that all the past came flooding back to me in a flash, but from that day forward I had a normal memory just like other people.

"Therefore if any man be in Christ, he is a new creature: old things are passed away; behold, all things are become new." 2 Corinthians 5:17[164]

'All' things. Praise the Lord. For me that meant *'all'* things; mental, emotional, physical, and spiritual. 'ALL' things! How can I not love and serve a living God who would take all my brokenness and inabilities and give me 'all things new'! My heart should ever bow before him day and night in gratitude for all His loving mercies! His praises ever on my lips. *HE IS ALIVE! HE IS TRUE! HIS MERCIES ABIDETH FOREVER! ...* **Praise the Lord!**

Hey, I don't know about you, but I have to stop here for a praise break.

Hallelujah!

Oh Lord, thou are merciful and kind, all blessings flow from you, my Lord. Glory! Glory to God most high! Father, I pray that these warm tears of love and gratitude falling down my cheeks and onto my sweater, melt my heart of all ungratefulness and pride, melt away all self-centeredness and vanity; for Lord, I am nothing, would be nothing, if it weren't for your loving mercy and grace. Oh Lord my God, be my all-in-all! Most holy Father, I pray that I may die daily that 'You' may live. Crucify this flesh and live anew in and through me, reach out to others through me. Oh my Lord and Father, that they may know You, Your love and mercies, as I have been permitted to know You. Open their spiritual eyes that they may see and know there is none like **YOU**. No one will love unconditionally like **YOU** No one will forgive like **YOU**. No one will understand and be compassionate like **YOU**. No one will always be with them, at their side, like **YOU**, for Your word says You will *'never'* leave us or forsake us. Hebrews 13:5b Oh my Lord. **THERE IS NONE LIKE YOU!**"

Let your conversation be without covetousness; and be content with such things as ye have: for he hath said, *I will never leave thee, nor forsake thee.* Hebrews 13:5.

Up to this point, the word 'I' has been used sparingly, writing in third person. It just didn't seem right to say 'I' when I was telling you about the events I could not remember, but have been told repeatedly by other family members. Things I know to be true from verifying reports of others outside the family; supporting events, and facts. But in this section, I have come to the place where *I can now speak from my own memories*; memories the Lord has allowed me to have of my very own. *PRAISE THE LORD*! What a wondrous God we serve!

Now, would you like to hear some of my 'personal' memories?

Are you sure? We could wait until a later time; I've already talked for quite a while today.

Okay. Well, I'm not saying there were absolutely 'no' memories from my childhood, there were about three or four, but I believe them to be spiritual memories, rather than typical memories.

Since I entered the first grade in 1948, it must have been either 1949 or 1950 when I dragged myself home from school one day and went to my mother asking if I could please lay down on their downstairs bed. My room was upstairs and the stairs were an overwhelming mountain I just couldn't climb right then. I remember lying on their bed, so sick and weak, feeling too depleted to even move or barely breathe. It's impossible to describe to you the feeling of sinking into a heavy exhaustion that pulled me deeper and deeper; the lack of strength or will to even speak.

As I lay on my left side, mindlessly staring out into the orchard between our house and the neighbor's house next door, I saw a small, misty, white, cloud-like image gently drift out of the trees. And I felt a warm soft breeze float in through the open window and kiss my face ever so gently, oh so slowly wrapping me all around in a soft caress; it felt as though I was being 'held' in gentle, loving arms, no longer even aware of the bed beneath me. As I lay in the arms of that gentle loving wind of our Lord, all exhaustion left my body, strength and peace seeped into every pore and thought. Even now, remembering, the word of our Lord fills my mind and soul. "Hast thou not known? hast thou not heard, that the everlasting God, the Lord, the Creator of the ends of the earth, fainteth not, neither is weary? there is no searching of his understanding. He giveth power to the faint; and to them that have no might he increaseth strength." Isaiah 40:28-29[165] "And he said unto me, My grace is sufficient for thee: for my strength is made perfect in weakness..." 2 Corinthians 12:9[166]

Still to this day, when I think about it, I can see the window and orchard spread out before me, and feel that gentle Spirit holding me, giving me strength. There have been days, times, I would have loved to be held in the arms of that gentle, strength-giving Spirit and be renewed in body and spirit again, just like He did that day. Gentle, warm tears trickle down my face as I remember the touch of His loving, strength-giving, healing embrace.

There were also a couple of experiences where I saw myself lying on the sofa or running down the walk to the outhouse. Another memory, one of my fondest, which may have been real, but felt so spiritual, was of watching myself sitting on the platform where the old, black, pot-bellied stove sat in the room between our living room and kitchen. The heat on my back was perfectly warm, not too hot, and the orange I was eating was so exquisite, it was like heaven to me; it felt like 'love'. As I watched this, I also could feel the heat and taste the orange. In fact, when I think about it, there are times I feel a tinge of that blessed heat and taste a hint of the orange in my mouth. To this very day my body craves heat on my back, that perfect heat, and the nectar of angels must surely be that heavenly scent and taste of a sweet juicy orange; my favorite fruit. Maurice, my father, told me much later in life he thinks that may have been Christmas, and that's all we had that year for Christmas; heat in the stove and a delicious orange. I believe he said someone had given us each an orange, but he wasn't sure.

Isn't it something that one of the hardest times of our lives became one of my greatest memories? Isn't that just like our God, to turn sadness into joy and lack into plenty? I was experiencing the bounty of heaven, and there was no sense or feeling of lack.

The Lord has been so gracious, I never 'experienced' the hard times or doing without, lived through them, but He washed the pain away with His presence and love.

There are times my heart goes out to those who have never done without or suffered hardship or pain; they have never known the supply our Lord gives to those in need. How our Lord turns a little into a lot and all stomachs are full and needs met - to feast on the manna of a heavenly orange or feel the heat of heaven warming your bones.

These, my dear friend, are my fondest memories; memories I wouldn't trade for all the gold in a thousand hills. While I am telling you about my spiritual memories, I would also like to tell you that is how I was able to talk when I couldn't hear, that, too, was a special gift from my heavenly Father. Oh, how I thank my Lord for being deaf! Without being deaf, there would have been several 'gifts' I would never have experienced; I would not have known what it was to live daily in the presence and care of my Lord, or what it was like to receive 'gifts' I did not earn or learn. I would not have been able to talk normally, read lips, or able to unconsciously 'read' the expressions and body language of others so acutely; it was as though those skills were born in me. No training or struggling to learn them on my part, just 'gifts of God'. Deeply, and oh so sincerely, I believe that ". . . we know that all things work together for good to them that love God, to them who are the called according to his purpose." Romans 8:28[167] "And God is able to make all grace abound toward you; that ye, always having all sufficiency in all things, may abound to every good work." 2 Corinthians 9:8[168]

I could tell you about the night I was so sad and despondent when I turned off my bedroom light and crawled into bed beside Lady, my Golden Sable (dog). And, in the dark of night a light came in my bedroom window and lit up the room with such a clear bright light, how all my sadness and despondency just washed away in its glow.

Remember my brother and me up in the barn hayloft? He was preaching and I was signing just like the lady I had seen in church. It turned out, that it wasn't 'play' signing, but the real thing. I had been blessed with the 'gift' of the deaf sign language, without being taught. When our Lord does something, He does it great! At the age of fourteen, I was asked to go to a college and 'help teach' signs to the students, and was also ask to travel with the Oral Roberts crusades interpreting for the deaf.

None of that had anything to do with me or my ability, it was God's gift, and its touching perfection. Truth be known, most of the time I 'let my hands do their thing' and I just knew what it meant, much like the time in 1983 when Gordon and I went to Germany. While he worked, I went to the library.

There in the library, I found, even though I had no knowledge of the German language, I knew what I was reading.

There was also the time I was substitute teaching a subject in the public school system on a mathematical problem I did not understand, under the anointing of the Holy Spirit. When the teacher returned to her class, she called and asked what I had done. She had been trying to teach that concept to her students for weeks and they just could not comprehend it. That, my friend, is a gift of the Holy Spirit; a gift dispersed when it's needed. All I did was do and say what the precious Spirit directed. To this day, I do not know how to work that mathematical problem.

I'll tell you one more. There were a couple times I tried to learn to play the piano, but it was useless. I was told it was probably because I was deaf in my early years. Rather than information going from my eyes to my brain like most 'normal' people, they believed information traveled a much longer route before it hit the brain and then started its way to the hands to respond. This is also the reason given for why I was a very slow reader and slow learner. But I truly believe my problem with playing the piano was not due to my slow learning, but because 'I was trying to do it myself, when I didn't need it'. It wasn't what I was meant to do.

Let me explain. We were attending a very small church in the rural Midwest one Sunday, where there was no piano or organ player to play for our service. The Holy Spirit nudged my heart and said, "Play the organ for the service". We had organ music for the service that day. I was playing the organ under the anointing for a church song service when I didn't know how to play. Later, my husband and others said, "I didn't know you knew how to play the organ." The only honest reply I could give them is, "I don't, but the Holy Spirit does." Before going on to another subject, I would like to mention something we all suffer from to some degree, and one of the biggest hindrances to the gifts of God on our lives: 'what will people think?' and 'what if I can't do it?' That's pride and vanity speaking in our mind. So, what if you can't do it? Will you die? Will the earth come to an end? We are afraid of being embarrassed or humiliated; we are thinking of ourselves. I cannot recall one time the Holy Spirit has prompted me to do or say something when He did not give the skill, strength, or knowledge to do it, when I act in obedience to His urging.

Have I ever heard the nudging of the Holy Spirit and sat there unmoved, have I ever been shown what He desires me to do and not do it?

Tearfully, I must say yes. But I try daily to crucify that part of my 'self' and surrender it to our precious Lord, to daily be better and more in tune with His will and His plan. It is my belief it is this obedience to His guidance that will make us able to be victorious in the last days. The word says 'even the elect'[169] would be deceived if our Lord did not quicken His return. The more I learn to listen and move in obedience, the more secure my blessed homecoming will be in our Lord. It is my belief those who live during the hard times to come will need to listen and obey the Spirit's leading just to survive. I praise our Lord that He allowed me to go through the things He did, that He used those means to teach me and guide me as a child into hearing and obeying His voice. It is His voice first heard, before ever hearing the sound of my mother, father, or brother. I am, and can do, nothing of any value in myself, but our Lord can give all talent and skill to whomsoever He chooses to do the work He chooses to be accomplished. We are but vessels in the hand of the potter. If we have allowed our clay to become dry and hardened, the Potter will search for another, more pliable, one who can be molded and shaped; one who will respond to His touch.

Oh Lord, my heart's cry is that I become more and more pliable in your hands, and all resistance or reluctance be worked out of me by Your patient shaping and corrections. Your gifts, talents, and knowledge can only be manifest through my emptiness and inability. Make me pliable to your will, purpose, and plan, for Your kingdom work and my life. For Lord, only through You am I able to be and do all things."[170]

To God be the glory for great things *'He' has done*! Praise the Lord our God, from whom all blessings, signs, wonders, and miracles, flow!

Oh, I would be remiss if I passed up the opportunity to give praise to my Lord for the births of my two sons; after being told having a child would likely cause my death, as well as the child's. The birth of our first son brought health to my body; all my health symptoms and problems vanished after my third month of pregnancy. And our second son was birthed in joyous giggles, born without one pain; he gently tickled me, and I laughed him into this world.

Remember my brother, Sonny, how he was stillborn, and when he came back to life my parents were told he would be very damaged, a vegetable? Well, when he was in the Navy and they ran their battery of tests, my parents were told he was the most intelligent person to have ever gone through there tests to date, he was a genius; a genius with a photographic memory.

There's more that could be told of events, visions and dreams. My father, a severely shy man, becoming a minister of our Lord's holy Word and pastoring a church, bodies made whole by the laying on of hands and prayer. And waking my husband up in the middle of the night to tell him the Holy Spirit said, 'If you want the baptism tonight, all you have to do is ask for it." He asked in a short, simple sentence and was filled with the Holy Spirit.

What was that scripture again, the one about...

"Jesus answered and said unto them, Verily I say unto you, If ye have faith, and doubt not, ye shall not only do this which is done to the fig tree, but also if ye shall say unto this mountain, Be thou removed, and be thou cast into the sea; it shall be done.

And all things, whatsoever ye shall ask in prayer, believing, ye shall receive." Matthew 21:21-22[171]

Let your heart be fed by 'His Word', guided by 'His Spirit' as you reach out, and claim all He has prepared for you.

"For there is no respect of persons with God." Romans 2:11[172]

"Jesus Christ the same yesterday, and today, and forever." Hebrews 13:8[173]

SUMMARY
~ 16 ~

. . . the Alpha and Omega, the beginning and the ending, saith the Lord, which is, and which was, and which is to come, the Almighty. Revelation 1:8

Herein is the purpose and goal of this book, to give all honor, praise, and glory to our Lord for great works **He** has done.

O give thanks to Jehovah call on His name Make known among the people His deed Sing to Him

Sing praise to Him tell of all His wonders
Glory in the name of His Holiness
Let rejoice the heart of those seeking Jehovah.
Seek Jehovah and His strength
seek His face continually
Remember His wonders that He has done
His signs and the judgments of His mouth
Sing to Jehovah all the earth

Proclaim the news from day to day of His salvation

Declare among the nations His glory
Among all the peoples His wonders
FOR ... GREAT IS JEHOVAH
and TO BE PRAISED GREATLY!"
I Chronicles 16:8-13, 23-25[174]

The Interlinear Hebrew Greek English Bible - Jay Green, general editor and translator 1976

"And the Spirit of God came upon Azariah the son of Oded: And he went out to meet Asa, and said unto him, Hear ye me, Asa, and all Judah and Benjamin; The Lord is with you, while ye be with him; and if ye seek him, he will be found of you; but if ye forsake him, he will forsake you. - But when they in their trouble did turn unto the Lord God of Israel, and sought him, he was found of them. - And they entered into a covenant to seek the Lord God of their fathers with all their heart and with all their soul; - And they sware unto the Lord with a loud voice, and with shouting, and with trumpets, and with cornets. And all Judah rejoiced at the oath: for they had sworn with all their heart, and sought him with their whole desire; and he was found of them: and the Lord gave them rest round about." 2 Chronicles 15:1-2, 4, 12, 14-15[175]

It is my heart's desire to learn from all those who have gone before and left a legacy of love for our God and examples to direct my path; remember the 'Steps'? They are a light unto my path of loving service and work for our precious Lord and Savior. I'm sure there are many more 'steps' we have overlooked as we skipped through their lives, but these are a good start.

1. Seek the Lord with all your heart and soul, fear the Lord your God and serve Him in truth with all your heart.
2. It isn't the denomination or the building you attend, it's the God you worship and serve, and how you seek Him that matters,
3. Be a genuine neighbor and friend.
4. Be a faithful prayer warrior on behalf of others.
5. Care and have concern for the needs of others above your own wants and desires.
6. Feed the hungry, give drink to the thirsty, take in the stranger, clothe the naked, visit the sick and those in prison.
7. Endure hardships, pain, and/or suffering while maintaining your deep heart-love for others and their needs.
8. Set your heart to understanding.
9. Be fully persuaded 'nothing' can separate you from the love of God.
10. Turn your eyes fully upon Jesus - focus on HIM.
11. Examine your heart, thoughts, and life, from the depth of your soul cry out, "Search me, Oh God".
12. Immediately, heed the voice of the Spirit.
13. Have a 'deep' Word-based, abiding faith in God.

The Word of the Spirit is the same to us as it was to Asa and all Judah and Benjamin, ***"Jehovah is with you when you are***

with Him, and if you seek him he shall be found of you. But if you forsake him he will forsake you ..."

"But they turned in their distress to Jehovah, the God of Israel, and ***they sought him* and he was found by them.** They entered into the covenant to seek Jehovah the God of their father with all their heart and with all their soul ... and they swore to Jehovah with a voice loud and with shouting and with trumpets and with ram's horns. And rejoiced all Judah on the oath for **with all their heart they had sworn,** and ***with all their desire they sought him*: and he was found by them,** and gave rest Jehovah to them all around."

> ***Seek ye the Lord while he may be found,***
> ***call ye upon him while he is near:***
>
> Isaiah 55:6[176]

ABOUT THE AUTHOR

ConnieJean started life fighting for one more hour, one more day, struggling to be like everyone else, to be normal; a fighter, one small step at a time, three steps forward and two steps back. She grew up with a knowledge of struggle and admiration for the quiet, determined ones ... for those who don't give up, those who make the best of the hand they were dealt.

She was a very blessed little girl who grew up in a family who came to know and love our Lord Jesus Christ, to know His deep love, compassion, and caring. A little girl who grew up in a time when the streets were safe and neighbors helped and cared for one another, when strangers were good and kind ... a new friend you were about to meet.

Bathed in God's love all her life, ConnieJean has been privileged to share His love and compassion, caring for all ages struggling heroically with physical, mental, and emotional handicaps ... burdens seemingly beyond endurance ... paraplegics, and those coming to the end of this life's journey; precious ones, our Father's jewels. She feels abundantly blessed by each one with whom she has had the privilege to share God's love by a tender touch, a compassionate listening ear, a smile, a laugh, a sincere hug.

ConnieJean is still married to her teenage heartthrob, deeply cherishes their two sons (Curtis and Randon), 5 grandchildren, and great grandchildren.

She is a credentialed minister with the Assemblies of God, and loves her Lord deeply, desiring to be in His presence and bask in His Word. She has held various positions of service including interpreting church services for the deaf, a gift from God at age 12, preaching by age 15, teaching all Sunday School class levels, filling in as interim minister between pastors, serving as youth pastor, and holding various church offices. ConnieJean feels privileged and blessed to have been used in the service of our God.

These have been –

Memoirs of such an Unworthy Child

I am not worthy of the least of all the mercies, And of all the truth, which thou hast shewed Unto thy servant; ...
Genesis 32:10 [KJV] [177]

Rev. ConnieJean Marquart-Harper
Email: Cj Hpr@msn.com   2serve@live.com
Webpage: www.106274.agwebservices1.org
National Evangelists Directory:
http://envangelists.ag.org/directory/
[ConnieJean Harper] **Text:** 1-260-242-6483

APPENDIX

SCRIPTURES & REFERENCES

Unless otherwise noted,
all scriptures have been taken from
Bible Explorer 4.0
Copyright © 2006 WORDsearch
www.bible-explorer.com

1. I am not worthy of the least of all the mercies, and of all the truth, which thou hast shewed unto thy servant. Genesis 32:10a (KJV)

2. Jesus answered and said unto them, Verily I say unto you, If ye have faith, and doubt not, ye shall not only do this which is done to the fig tree, but also if ye shall say unto this mountain, Be thou removed, and be thou cast into the sea; it shall be done. And all things, whatsoever ye shall ask in prayer, believing, ye shall receive. Matthew 21:21-22 (KJV)

3. Beloved, if our heart condemn us not, then have we confidence toward God. And whatsoever we ask, we receive of him, because we keep his commandments, and do those things that are pleasing in his sight. 1 John 3:21-22 (KJV)

4. And he said unto them, Go ye into all the world, and preach the gospel to every creature. He that believeth and is baptized shall be saved; but he that believeth not shall be damned. And these signs shall follow them that believe; In my name shall they cast out devils; they shall speak with new tongues;

They shall take up serpents; and if they drink any deadly thing, it shall not hurt them; they shall lay hands on the sick, and they shall recover . . And they went forth, and preached everywhere, the Lord working with them, and confirming the word with signs following. Amen. Mark 16:15-18, 20 (KJV)

5. For there is no respect of persons with God. Romans 2:11 (KJV)

6. Jesus Christ the same yesterday, and today, and forever. Hebrews 13:8 (KJV)

MAURICE'S MIRACLE

7. But if from thence thou shalt seek the Lord thy God, thou shalt find him, if thou seek him with all thy heart and with all thy soul. Deuteronomy 4:29 (KJV)

8. Only fear the Lord, and serve him in truth with all your heart: for consider how great things he hath done for you. 1 Samuel 12:24 KJV)

9. See then that ye walk circumspectly, not as fools, but as wise, redeeming the time, because the days are evil. Wherefore be ye not unwise, but understanding what the will of the Lord is. And be not drunk with wine, wherein is excess; but be filled with the Spirit; Ephesians 5:15-18 (KJV)

10. And the serpent said unto the woman, Ye shall not surely die: For God doth know that in the day ye eat thereof, then your eyes shall be opened, and ye shall be as gods, knowing good and evil. And when the woman saw that the tree was good for food, and that it was pleasant to the eyes, and a tree to be desired to make one wise, she took of the fruit thereof, and did eat, and gave also unto her husband with her; and he did eat. Genesis 3:4-6 (KJV)

11. ...take heed lest by any means this liberty of yours become a stumbling block to them that are weak. 1 Corinthians 8:9 (KJV)

12. Let us not therefore judge one another anymore: but judge this rather, that no man put a stumbling block or an occasion to fall in his brother's way. Romans 14:13 (KJV)

13. He that loveth his brother abideth in the light, and there is none occasion of stumbling in him. 1 John 2:10 (KJV)

14. Then spake Jesus again unto them, saying, I am the light of the world: he that followeth me shall not walk in darkness, but shall have the light of life. John 8:12 (KJV)

15. And he that taketh not his cross, and followeth after me, is not worthy of me. He that findeth his life shall lose it: and he that loseth his life for my sake shall find it. Matthew 10:38-39 (KJV)

16. For in him we live, and move, and have our being; as certain also of your own poets have said, For we are also his off spring. Acts 17:28 (KJV)

17. For I have given you an example, that ye should do as I have done to you. John 13:15 (KJV)

18. And the King shall answer and say unto them, Verily I say unto you, Inasmuch as ye have done *it* unto one of the least of these my brethren, ye have done *it* unto me. Matt 25:40 (KJV)

19. For the kingdom of heaven is as a man travelling into a far country who called his own servants, and delivered unto them his goods. And unto one he gave five talents, to another two, and to another one; to every man according to his several ability; and straightway took his journey. Then he that had received the five talents went and traded with the same, and made them other five talents. And likewise he that had received two, he also gained other two. But he that had received one went and digged in the earth, and hid his lord's money. After a long time the lord of those servants cometh, and reckoneth with them. And so he that had received five talents came and brought other five talents, saying, Lord, thou deliveredst unto me five talents: behold, I have gained

beside them five talents more. His lord said unto him, Well done, thou good and faithful servant: thou hast been faithful over a few things, I will make thee ruler over many things: enter thou into the joy of thy lord. He also that had received two talents came and said, Lord, thou deliveredst unto me two talents: behold, I have gained two other talents beside them. His lord said unto him, Well done, good and faithful servant; thou hast been faithful over a few things, I will make thee ruler over many things: enter thou into the joy of thy lord. Then he which had received the one talent came and said, Lord, I knew thee that thou art an hard man, reaping where thou hast not sown, and gathering where thou hast not strawed: And I was afraid, and went and hid thy talent in the earth: lo, there thou hast that is thine. His lord answered and said unto him, Th ou wicked and slothful servant, thou knewest that I reap where I sowed not, and gather where I have not strawed: Th ou oughtest therefore to have put my money to the exchangers, and then at my coming I should have received mine own with usury. Take therefore the talent from him, and give it unto him which hath ten talents. For unto every one that hath shall be given, and he shall have abundance: but from him that hath not shall be taken away even that which he hath. And cast ye the unprofitable servant into outer darkness: there shall be weeping and gnashing of teeth. Matthew 25:14-30 (KJV)

20. If any of you lack wisdom, let him ask of God, that giveth to all men liberally, and upbraideth not; and it shall be given him. James 1:5 (KJV)

21. Charge them that are rich in this world, that they be not high minded, nor trust in uncertain riches, but in the living God, who giveth us richly all things to enjoy; 1 Timothy 6:17 (KJV)

22. For I was an hungred, and ye gave me meat: I was thirsty, and ye gave me drink: I was a stranger, and ye took me in: Naked, and ye clothed me: I was sick, and ye visited me: I was in prison, and ye came unto me. Then shall the righteous answer him,

saying, Lord, when saw we thee an hungred, and fed thee? or thirsty, and gave thee drink? When saw we thee a stranger, and took thee in? or naked, and clothed thee? Or when saw we thee sick, or in prison, and came unto thee? And the King shall answer and say unto them, Verily I say unto you, Inasmuch as ye have done it unto one of the least of these my brethren, ye have done it unto me. Matthew 25:35-40 (KJV)

23. What doth it profit, my brethren, though a man say he hath faith, and have not works? can faith save him? If a brother or sister be naked, and destitute of daily food, And one of you say unto them, Depart in peace, be ye warmed and filled; notwithstanding ye give them not those things which are needful to the body; what doth it profit? Even so faith, if it hath not works, is dead, being alone. James 2:14-17 (KJV)

24. Train up a child in the way he should go: and when he is old, he will not depart from it. Proverbs 22:6 (KJV)

25. And when the woman saw that the tree *was* good for food, and that it *was* pleasant to the eyes, and a tree to be desired to make *one* wise, she took of the fruit thereof, and did eat, and gave also unto her husband with her; and he did eat. Gen 3:6 (KJV)

26. He that loveth his brother abideth in the light, and there is none occasion of stumbling in him. 1 John 2:10 (KJV)

27. And the King shall answer and say unto them, Verily I say unto you, Inasmuch as ye have done *it* unto one of the least of these my brethren, ye have done *it* unto me. Matt 25:40 (KJV)

28. Even so faith, if it hath not works, is dead, being alone. James 2:17 (KJV)

29. And I will forsake the remnant of mine inheritance, and deliver them into the hand of their enemies; and they shall become a prey and a spoil to all their enemies; Because they have done that which was evil in my sight, and have provoked

me to anger, since the day their fathers came forth out of Egypt, even unto this day. 2 Kings 21:14-15 (KJV)

SONNY'S FIRST CRY

30. And the Lord appeared unto him in the plains of Mamre: and he sat in the tent door in the heat of the day; And he lift up his eyes and looked, and, lo, three men stood by him: and when he saw them, he ran to meet them from the tent door, and bowed himself toward the ground, And said, My Lord, if now I have found favour in thy sight, pass not away, I pray thee, from thy servant: Genesis 18:1-3 (KJV) And they said unto him, Where is Sarah thy wife? And he said, Behold, in the tent. And he said, I will certainly return unto thee according to the time of life; and, lo, Sarah thy wife shall have a son. And Sarah heard it in the tent door, which was behind him. Genesis 18:9-10 (KJV)

31. Jesus said unto them, Verily, verily, I say unto you, Before Abraham was, I am. John 8:58 (KJV) Jesus Christ the same yesterday, and today, and forever. Hebrews 13:8 (KJV) Verily, verily, I say unto you, He that believeth on me, the works that I do shall he do also; and greater works than these shall he do; because I go unto my Father. And whatsoever ye shall ask in my name, that will I do, that the Father may be glorified in the Son. If ye shall ask any thing in my name, I will do it. John 14:12-14 (KJV) At that day ye shall know that I am in my Father, and ye in me, and I in you. He that hath my commandments, and keepeth them, he it is that loveth me: and he that loveth me shall be loved of my Father, and I will love him, and will manifest myself to him. John 14:20-21 (KJV)

32. But glory, honour, and peace, to every man that worketh good, to the Jew first, and also to the Gentile: For there is no respect of persons with God. Romans 2:10-11 (KJV)

33. And he said unto me, O Daniel, a man greatly beloved, understand the words that I speak unto thee, and stand

upright: for unto thee am I now sent. And when he had spoken this word unto me, I stood trembling. Then said he unto me, Fear not, Daniel: for from the first day that thou didst set thine heart to understand, and to chasten thyself before thy God, thy words were heard, and I am come for thy words. Daniel 10:11-12 (KJV)

34. Chorus "Let Me Touch Him" – Russell Mauldin A story was told about the gentleman who wrote the song; it was said the first time he sang the song people came up to him after the service and asked where the choir was located. He told them there was no choir. They then asked if he had a tape with a choir singing as backup music. He said there was no choir and no backup music. He was then told … there was a choir, a heavenly choir singing the song with him.

35. As many as I love, I rebuke and chasten: be zealous therefore, and repent. Behold, I stand at the door, and knock: if any man hear my voice, and open the door, I will come in to him, and will sup with him, and he with me. To him that overcometh will I grant to sit with me in my throne, even as I also overcame, and am set down with my Father in his throne. He that hath an ear, let him hear what the Spirit saith unto the churches. Revelation 3:19-22 (KJV)

36. Greater love hath no man than this, that a man lay down his life for his friends. John 15:13 (KJV)

37. Thou shalt also consider in thine heart, that, as a man chasteneth his son, so the Lord thy God chasteneth thee. Therefore thou shalt keep the commandments of the Lord thy God, to walk in his ways, and to fear him. Deuteronomy 8:5-6 (KJV) [God's word to David concerning his seed, son.] I will be his father, and he shall be my son. If he commit iniquity, I will chasten him with the rod of men, and with the stripes of the children of men: But my mercy shall not depart away from him, as I took it from Saul, whom I put away before thee. 2 Samuel 7:14-15 (KJV) Behold, happy is the man whom

God correcteth: therefore despise not thou the chastening of the Almighty: For he maketh sore, and bindeth up: he woundeth, and his hands make whole. Job 5:17-18 (KJV) See 35 Revelation 3:19-21 (KJV)

38. Charles G. Finney – [www.whatsaiththescripture.com/Voice/Oberlin 1856/OE1856.Believing.Heart.html] The Oberlin Evangelist by Charles G Finney; 1856; Lecture VIII; "On Believing with The Heart".

39. Cecil J Carter [?] [http://truthinheart.com/EarlyOberlinCD/CD/Finney/OE/561203 believing w heart.htm] "On Believing With The Heart"; December 3, 1856; By The Rev. CHARLES G. FINNEY

40. Charles G. Finney – 'A Treasury of Great Preaching'

41. And we know that all things work together for good to them that love God, to them who are the called according to *his* purpose. Romans 8:28 (KJV)

42. Then said Jesus to those Jews which believed on him, If ye continue in my word, then are ye my disciples indeed; And ye shall know the truth, and the truth shall make you free. John 8:31-32 (KJV)

A DEVASTATING DILEMMA
AGAINST ALL ODDS

43. For my thoughts are not your thoughts, neither are your ways my ways, saith the Lord. For as the heavens are higher than the earth, so are my ways higher than your ways, and my thoughts than your thoughts. Isaiah 55:8-9 (KJV)

44. For this thing I besought the Lord thrice, that it might depart from me. And he said unto me, My grace is sufficient for thee: for my strength is made perfect in weakness. Most gladly therefore will I rather glory in my infirmities, that the power of Christ may rest upon me. Therefore I take pleasure in

infirmities, in reproaches, in necessities, in persecutions, in distresses for Christ's sake: for when I am weak, then am I strong. 2 Corinthian 12:8-10 (KJV)

45. For this thing I besought the Lord thrice, that it might depart from me. And he said unto me, My grace is sufficient for thee: for my strength is made perfect in weakness. Most gladly therefore will I rather glory in my infirmities, that the power of Christ may rest upon me. Therefore I take pleasure in infirmities, in reproaches, in necessities, in persecutions, in distresses for Christ's sake: for when I am weak, then am I strong. 2 Corinthian 12:8-10 (KJV)

46. And Balaam rose up in the morning, and saddled his ass, and went with the princes of Moab. And God's anger was kindled because he went: and the angel of the Lord stood in the way for an adversary against him. Now he was riding upon his ass, and his two servants were with him. And the ass saw the angel of the Lord standing in the way, and his sword drawn in his hand: and the ass turned aside out of the way, and went into the field: and Balaam smote the ass, to turn her into the way. But the angel of the Lord stood in a path of the vineyards, a wall being on this side, and a wall on that side. And when the ass saw the angel of the Lord, she throughst herself unto the wall, and crushed Balaam's foot against the wall: and he smote her again. And the angel of the Lord went further, and stood in a narrow place, where was no way to turn either to the right hand or to the left. And when the ass saw the angel of the Lord, she fell down under Balaam: and Balaam's anger was kindled, and he smote the ass with a staff. And the Lord opened the mouth of the ass, and she said unto Balaam, What have I done unto thee, that thou hast smitten me these three times? And Balaam said unto the ass, Because thou hast mocked me: I would there were a sword in mine hand, for now would I kill thee. And the ass said unto Balaam, Am not I thine ass, upon which thou hast ridden ever since I was thine unto this day? was I ever wont to do so

unto thee? And he said, Nay. Then the Lord opened the eyes of Balaam, and he saw the angel of the Lord standing in the way, and his sword drawn in his hand: and he bowed down his head, and fell flat on his face. And the angel of the Lord said unto him, Wherefore hast thou smitten thine ass these three times? behold, I went out to withstand thee, because thy way is perverse before me: Numbers 22:21-32 (KJV)

47. For this thing I besought the Lord thrice, that it might depart from me. And he said unto me, My grace is sufficient for thee: for my strength is made perfect in weakness. Most gladly therefore will I rather glory in my infirmities, that the power of Christ may rest upon me. Therefore I take pleasure in infirmities, in reproaches, in necessities, in persecutions, in distresses for Christ's sake: for when I am weak, then am I strong. 2 Cor 12:810 (KJV)

48. He must increase, but I must decrease. John 3:30 (KJV)

49. Trust in the Lord with all thine heart; and lean not unto thine own understanding. Prov 3:5 (KJV)

50. I say unto you, that likewise joy shall be in heaven over one sinner that repenteth, more than over ninety and nine just persons, which need no repentance. Luke 15:7 (KJV)

51. Be strong and of a good courage, fear not, nor be afraid of them: for the Lord thy God, he it is that doth go with thee; he will not fail thee, nor forsake thee. Deuteronomy 31:6 (KJV) And Jehovah, he it is that goeth before thee: he will be with thee; he will not leave thee, nor forsake thee; fear not, neither be dismayed. Deuteronomy 31:8 (Darby)

52. nd I will make an everlasting covenant with them, that I will not turn away from them, to do them good; but I will put my fear in their hearts, that they shall not depart from me. Jeremiah 32:40 (KJV)

53. For I am persuaded, that neither death, nor life, nor angels, nor principalities, nor powers, nor things present, nor things to come, Nor height, nor depth, nor any other creature, shall be able to separate us from the love of God, which is in Christ Jesus our Lord. Romans 8:38-39 (KJV)

54. But when Jesus heard it, he answered him, saying, Fear not: believe only, and she shall be made whole. Luke 8:50 (KJV)

55. In him was life; and the life was the light of men. John 1:4 (KJV)

'KABOOSKI' and 'KANEKA'

56. "Turn Your Eyes Upon Jesus" by Helen H Lemmel The Story Behind the Hymn [http://bigchurch.com/blog/444/ post 120106.html]

57. But the ship was now in the midst of the sea, tossed with waves: for the wind was contrary. And in the fourth watch of the night Jesus went unto them, walking on the sea. And when the disciples saw him walking on the sea, they were troubled, saying, It is a spirit; and they cried out for fear. But straightway Jesus spake unto them, saying, Be of good cheer; it is I; be not afraid. And Peter answered him and said, Lord, if it be thou, bid me come unto thee on the water. And he said, Come. And when Peter was come down out of the ship, he walked on the water, to go to Jesus. But when he saw the wind boisterous, he was afraid; and beginning to sink, he cried, saying, Lord, save me. And immediately Jesus stretched forth his hand, and caught him, and said unto him, O thou of little faith, wherefore didst thou doubt? And when they were come into the ship, the wind ceased. Matthew 14:24-32 (KJV) Let your moderation be known unto all men. The Lord is at hand. Be careful for nothing; but in every thing by prayer and supplication with thanksgiving let your requests be made known unto God. And the peace of God, which passeth all understanding, shall keep your hearts and minds through Christ Jesus. Finally, brethren, whatsoever things

are true, whatsoever things are honest, whatsoever things are just, whatsoever things are pure, whatsoever things are lovely, whatsoever things are of good report; if there be any virtue, and if there be any praise, think on these things. Th ose things, which ye have both learned, and received, and heard, and seen in me, do: and the God of peace shall be with you. Philippians 4:5-9 (KJV) Thou wilt keep him in perfect peace, whose mind is stayed on thee: because he trusteth in thee. Trust ye in the Lord for ever: for in the Lord JEHOVAH is everlasting strength: Isaiah 26:3-4 (KJV)

58. "And the peace of God, which passeth all understanding, shall keep your hearts and minds through Christ Jesus." Phil 4:7 (KJV)

59. Finally, brethren, farewell. Be perfect, be of good comfort, be of one mind, live in peace; and the God of love and peace shall be with you. 2 Corinthians 13:11 (KJV)

60. And we know that all things work together for good to them that love God, to them who are the called according to *his* purpose. Romans 8:28 (KJV)

61. Now faith is the substance of things hoped for, the evidence of things not seen. Hebrews 11:1 (KJV)

62. Be not forgetful to entertain strangers: for thereby some have entertained angels unawares. Heb 13:2 (KJV)

63. Beloved, think it not strange concerning the fiery trial which is to try you, as though some strange thing happened unto you: But rejoice, inasmuch as ye are partakers of Christ's sufferings; that, when his glory shall be revealed, ye may be glad also with exceeding joy. 1 Peter 4:12-13 (KJV)

A PRICE WORTH PAYING?

64. And the serpent said unto the woman, Ye shall not surely die: 5 For God doth know that in the day ye eat thereof, then your

eyes shall be opened, and ye shall be as gods, knowing good and evil. Gen 3:4-5 (KJV)

65. For the wrath of God is revealed from heaven against all ungodliness and unrighteousness of men, who hold the truth in unrighteousness; Because that which may be known of God is manifest in them; for God hath shewed it unto them. For the invisible things of him from the creation of the world are clearly seen, being understood by the things that are made, even his eternal power and Godhead; so that they are without excuse: Because that, when they knew God, they glorified him not as God, neither were thankful; but became vain in their imaginations, and their foolish heart was darkened. Professing themselves to be wise, they became fools, And changed the glory of the uncorruptible God into an image made like to corruptible man, and to birds, and four footed beasts, and creeping things. Romans 1:18-23 (KJV)

66. My son, forget not my law; but let thine heart keep my commandments: For length of days, and long life, and peace, shall they add to thee. Let not mercy and truth forsake thee: bind them about thy neck; write them upon the table of thine heart: So shalt thou find favour and good understanding in the sight of God and man. Trust in the Lord with all thine heart; and lean not unto thine own understanding. In all thy ways acknowledge him, and he shall direct thy paths. Proverbs 3:1-6 (KJV)

67. Therefore take no thought, saying, What shall we eat? or, What shall we drink? or, Wherewithal shall we be clothed? 32 (For after all these things do the Gentiles seek:) for your heavenly Father knoweth that ye have need of all these things. 33 But seek ye first the kingdom of God, and his righteousness; and all these things shall be added unto you. Matthew 6:31-33 (KJV)

68. For whosoever shall do the will of God, the same is my brother, and my sister, and mother. Mark 3:35 (KJV)

69. But when Jesus saw *it*, he was much displeased, and said unto them, Suffer the little children to come unto me, and forbid them not: for of such is the kingdom of God. Mark 10:14 (KJV)

70. For God so loved the world, that he gave his only begotten Son, that whosoever believeth in him should not perish, but have everlasting life. John 3:16 (KJV)

71. Now the God of patience and consolation grant you to be likeminded one toward another according to Christ Jesus: That ye may with one mind *and* one mouth glorify God, even the Father of our Lord Jesus Christ. Romans 15:5-6 (KJV) But if we hope for that we see not, then do we with patience wait for it. Romans 8:25 (KJV)

72. For God so loved the world, that he gave his only begotten Son, that whosoever believeth in him should not perish, but have everlasting life. John 3:16 (KJV)Now the God of hope fill you with all joy and peace in believing, that ye may abound in hope, through the power of the Holy Ghost. Romans 15:13 (KJV)

73. "Blessed *be* God, even the Father of our Lord Jesus Christ, the Father of mercies, and the God of all comfort;" 2 Cor 1:3 (KJV)

74. Finally, brethren, farewell. Be perfect, be of good comfort, be of one mind, live in peace; and the God of love and peace shall be with you. 2 Cor 13:11 (KJV)

75. "And we know that all things work together for good to them that love God, to them who are the called according to *his* purpose." Romans 8:28 (KJV)

76. There shall not any man be able to stand before thee all the days of thy life: as I was with Moses, so I will be with thee: I will not fail thee, nor forsake thee. Joshua 1:5 (KJV)

77. That it might be fulfilled which was spoken by Esaias the prophet, saying, Himself took our infirmities, and bare our sicknesses. Matthew 8:17 (KJV)

78. Therefore his sisters sent unto him, saying, Lord, behold, he whom thou lovest is sick. **4** When Jesus heard *that*, he said, This sickness is not unto death, but for the glory of God, that the Son of God might be glorified thereby. John 11:3-4 (KJV)

79. (It was that Mary which anointed the Lord with ointment, and wiped his feet with her hair, whose brother Lazarus was sick.) Therefore his sisters sent unto him, saying, Lord, behold, he whom thou lovest is sick. When Jesus heard that, he said, This sickness is not unto death, but for the glory of God, that the Son of God might be glorified thereby. John 11:2-4 (KJV)

80. Are they ministers of Christ? (I speak as a fool) I am more; in labours more abundant, in stripes above measure, in prisons more frequent, in deaths oft. Of the Jews five times received I forty stripes save one. Thrice was I beaten with rods, once was I stoned, thrice I suffered shipwreck, a night and a day I have been in the deep; In journeyings often, in perils of waters, in perils of robbers, in perils by mine own countrymen, in perils by the heathen, in perils in the city, in perils in the wilderness, in perils in the sea, in perils among false brethren; In weariness and painfulness, in watchings often, in hunger and thirst, in fastings often, in cold and nakedness. Beside those things that are without, that which cometh upon me daily, the care of all the churches. Who is weak, and I am not weak? who is offended, and I burn not? If I must needs glory, I will glory of the things which concern mine infirmities. The God and Father of our Lord Jesus Christ, which is blessed for evermore, knoweth that I lie not. 2 Corinthians 11:23-31 (KJV)

81. Of such an one will I glory: yet of myself I will not glory, but in mine infirmities. 2 Corinthians 12:5 (KJV)

82. And lest I should be exalted above measure through the abundance of the revelations, there was given to me a thorn in the flesh, the messenger of Satan to buffet me, lest I should be exalted above measure. For this thing I besought the Lord thrice, that it might depart from me. And he said unto me,

My grace is sufficient for thee: for my strength is made perfect in weakness. Most gladly therefore will I rather glory in my infirmities, that the power of Christ may rest upon me. 2 Corinthians 12:7-9 (KJV)

83. Therefore I take pleasure in infirmities, in reproaches, in necessities, in persecutions, in distresses for Christ's sake: for when I am weak, then am I strong. 2 Cor 12:10 (KJV)

84. For this thing I besought the Lord thrice, that it might depart from me. 2 Cor 12:8 (KJV)

85. Strong's Talking Greek & Hebrew Dictionary; Bible Explorer 4.0; Copyright © 2006 WORDsearch; www.bible-explorer.com

86. And lest I should be exalted above measure through the abundance of the revelations, there was given to me a thorn in the flesh, the messenger of Satan to buffet me, lest I should be exalted above measure. For this thing I besought the Lord thrice, that it might depart from me. And he said unto me, My grace is sufficient for thee: for my strength is made perfect in weakness. Most gladly therefore will I rather glory in my infirmities, that the power of Christ may rest upon me. 2 Cor 12:7-9 (KJV)

87. And he said unto me, My grace is sufficient for thee: for my strength is made perfect in weakness. 2 Cor 12:9 (KJV)

88. Search me, O God, and know my heart: try me, and know my thoughts: And see if there be any wicked way in me, and lead me in the way everlasting. Psalms 139:23-24 (KJV)

89. For I know that in me (that is, in my flesh,) dwelleth no good thing: for to will is present with me; but how to perform that which is good I find not. For the good that I would I do not: but the evil which I would not, that I do. Romans 7:18-19 (KJV)

90. Examine yourselves, whether ye be in the faith; prove your own selves. Know ye not your own selves, how that Jesus Christ is in you, except ye be reprobates? 2 Corinthians 13:5 (KJV)

91. I can do all things through Christ which strengtheneth me. Philippians 4:13 (KJV)

92. I am crucified with Christ: nevertheless I live; yet not I, but Christ liveth in me: and the life which I now live in the flesh I live by the faith of the Son of God, who loved me, and gave himself for me. Galatians 2:20 (KJV)

AND THE MORTARS FELL

93. A thousand shall fall at thy side, and ten thousand at thy right hand; but it shall not come nigh thee. Psalms 91:7 (KJV)

94. The Lord is thy keeper: the Lord is thy shade upon thy right hand. The sun shall not smite thee by day, nor the moon by night. The Lord shall preserve thee from all evil: he shall preserve thy soul. The Lord shall preserve thy going out and thy coming in from this time forth, and even for evermore. Psalms 121:5-8 (KJV)

95. But Jesus beheld them, and said unto them, With men this is impossible; but with God all things are possible. Matthew 19:26 (KJV)

96. And he said, Abba, Father, all things are possible unto thee; take away this cup from me: nevertheless not what I will, but what thou wilt. Mark 14:36 (KJV)

97. Chorus "What a Mighty God We Serve" lyrics provided by Hezekiah Walker [http://www.allgospellyrics.com/?sec=listing&lyricid=1084] What a Mighty God We Serve! Clara M. Brooks / B.E. Warren

98. The story behind this song is an interesting glimpse into the life of Barney Warren. Axchie A. Bolitho writes: "In the music room of what is now Anderson College and Theological Seminary, a committee was hard at work on a new song book. Mr. Warren's thoughts slipped away from notes and scales and bars and rested for a time on the Creator and the

world He has made; the majestic Rockies, the far reaches of the plains, the oceans bounding the continents, rivers flowing to the sea, fruitful valleys feeding man and beast, the immensities of those other universes of which we know so little – and above all – God. Overwhelmed with wonder and awe, he became aware of a melody forming in his mind. Turning to Mrs. Brooks who was helping with the composing, he described as best he could what he had just seen and felt, and then sang the tune to which no words had come. As Mrs. Brooks listened, her face lighted up and she exclaimed: 'Why the chorus seems to say, what a mighty God we serve.' Very shortly she had written the verses and the quartet had a new song." This song has since become one of the "standards" of the church. [http:// projectfoundations.weebly.com/song-listing--stories.html]

99. "His Name is Wonderful" by Audrey Mieir [http://www.faithclipart.com/guide/Christian-Music/hymns-the-songs-and-the-stories/his-name-is-wonderful-the-song-and-the-story.html] For unto us a child is born, unto us a son is given: and the government shall be upon his shoulder: and his name shall be called Wonderful, Counsellor, The mighty God, The everlasting Father, The Prince of Peace. Isaiah 9:6 (KJV)

100. "The Healing Waters Flow" by: H.H. Heimar, L.L. Pickett 1951

LED BY A CHILD

101. Be sober, be vigilant; because your adversary the devil, as a roaring lion, walketh about, seeking whom he may devour: 1 Peter 5:8 (KJV)

102. If my people, which are called by my name, shall humble themselves, and pray, and seek my face, and turn from their wicked ways; then will I hear from heaven, and will forgive their sin, and will heal their land. Now mine eyes shall be open, and mine ears attent unto the prayer that is made in this place. For now have I chosen and sanctified this house,

that my name may be there for ever: and mine eyes and mine heart shall be there perpetually. 2 Chronicles 7:14-16 (KJV)

103. But Jesus said, Suffer little children, and forbid them not, to come unto me: for of such is the kingdom of heaven. Matthew 19:14 (KJV) But when Jesus saw it, he was much displeased, and said unto them, Suffer the little children to come unto me, and forbid them not: for of such is the kingdom of God. Mark 10:14-15 (KJV) But Jesus called them unto him, and said, Suffer little children to come unto me, and forbid them not: for of such is the kingdom of God. Luke 18:16 (KJV)

104. Be sober, be vigilant; because your adversary the devil, as a roaring lion, walketh about, seeking whom he may devour: 1 Peter 5:8 (KJV)

105. But when Jesus saw it, he was much displeased, and said unto them, Suffer the little children to come unto me, and forbid them not: for of such is the kingdom of God. Verily I say unto you, Whosoever shall not receive the kingdom of God as a little child, he shall not enter therein. Mark 10:14-15 (KJV)

106. Who shall separate us from the love of Christ? *shall* tribulation, or distress, or persecution, or famine, or nakedness, or peril, or sword? As it is written, For thy sake we are killed all the day long; we are accounted as sheep for the slaughter. Nay, in all these things we are more than conquerors through him that loved us. For I am persuaded, that neither death, nor life, nor angels, nor principalities, nor powers, nor things present, nor things to come, Nor height, nor depth, nor any other creature, shall be able to separate us from the love of God, which is in Christ Jesus our Lord. Romans 8:35-39 (KJV)

107. But Jesus beheld *them*, and said unto them, With men this is impossible; but with God all things are possible. Matt 19:26 (KJV)

108. Jesus said unto him, If thou canst believe, all things are possible to him that believeth. Mark 9:23 (KJV)

109. And Jesus looking upon them saith, With men it is impossible, but not with God: for with God all things are possible. Mark 10:27 (KJV)

110. And he that searcheth the hearts knoweth what is the mind of the Spirit, because he maketh intercession for the saints according to the will of God. And we know that all things work together for good to them that love God, to them who are the called according to his purpose. Romans 8:27-28 (KJV)

111. And God is able to make all grace abound toward you; that ye, always having all sufficiency in all things, may abound to every good work: 2 Corinthians 9:8 (KJV)

112. And you will again give ear to the voice of the Lord, and do all his orders which I have given you today. And the Lord your God will make you fertile in all good things, blessing the work of your hands, and the fruit of your body, and the fruit of your cattle, and the fruit of your land: for the Lord will have joy in you, as he had in your fathers: If you give ear to the voice of the Lord your God, keeping his orders and his laws which are recorded in this book of the law, and turning to the Lord your God with all your heart and with all your soul. Deuteronomy 30:8-10 (BBE)

"2 . . . 4 . . . 6eeeee . . . JUMP!"

113. And the spirit of the Lord shall rest upon him, the spirit of wisdom and understanding, the spirit of counsel and might, the spirit of knowledge and of the fear of the Lord; And shall make him of quick understanding in the fear of the Lord: and he shall not judge after the sight of his eyes, neither reprove after the hearing of his ears: But with righteousness shall he judge the poor, and reprove with equity for the meek of the earth: and he shall smite the earth with the rod of his mouth, and with the breath of his lips shall he slay the wicked. And righteousness shall be the girdle of his loins, and faithfulness the girdle of his reins. The wolf also shall dwell with the lamb,

and the leopard shall lie down with the kid; and the calf and the young lion and the fatling together; and a little child shall lead them. Isaiah 11:2-6 (KJV)

114. The wolf also shall dwell with the lamb, ... Isaiah 11:6 (KJV)

115. ... and the leopard shall lie down with the kid; ... Isaiah 11:6 (KJV)

116. ... and the calf and the young lion and the fatling together; ... Isaiah 11:6

117. The wolf also shall dwell with the lamb, and the leopard shall lie down with the kid; and the calf and the young lion and the fatling together; and a little child shall lead them. Isaiah 11:6

118. But when Jesus saw *it*, he was much displeased, and said unto them, Suffer the little children to come unto me, and forbid them not: for of such is the kingdom of God. Verily I say unto you, Whosoever shall not receive the kingdom of God as a little child, he shall not enter therein. Mark 10:14-15 (KJV)

119. Search me, O God, and know my heart: try me, and know my thoughts: And see if *there be any* wicked way in me, and lead me in the way everlasting. Psalms 139:23-24 (KJV)

120. Ye ask, and receive not, because ye ask amiss, that ye may consume it upon your lusts. James 4:3 (KJV)

121. Draw nigh to God, and he will draw nigh to you. Cleanse your hands, ye sinners; and purify your hearts, ye double minded. Be afflicted, and mourn, and weep: let your laughter be turned to mourning, and your joy to heaviness. Humble yourselves in the sight of the Lord, and he shall lift you up. James 4:8-10 (KJV)

122. For the invisible things of him from the creation of the world are clearly seen, being understood by the things that are made, *even* his eternal power and Godhead; so that they are without excuse: Romans 1:20 (KJV)

'JUST KEEP LOVIN'

123. Thus saith the Lord, thy redeemer, and he that formed thee from the womb, I am the Lord that maketh all things; that stretcheth forth the heavens alone; that spreadeth abroad the earth by myself; Isaiah 44:24 (KJV)

124. Before I formed thee in the belly I knew thee; and before thou camest forth out of the womb I sanctified thee, and I ordained thee a prophet unto the nations. Jeremiah 1:5 (KJV)

125. By their fruits ye shall know them. Do *men* gather grapes of thorns, or figs of thistles? Even so every good tree bringeth forth good fruit; but the corrupt tree bringeth forth evil fruit. A good tree cannot bring forth evil fruit, neither can a corrupt tree bring forth good fruit. Every tree that bringeth not forth good fruit is hewn down, and cast into the fire. Therefore by their fruits ye shall know them. Matt 7:16-20 (ASV)

126. Even a child is known by his doings, whether his work be pure, and whether it be right. Proverbs 20:11 (KJV)

127. My son, forget not my law; but let thine heart keep my commandments: For length of days, and long life, and peace, shall they add to thee. Let not mercy and truth forsake thee: bind them about thy neck; write them upon the table of thine heart: So shalt thou find favour and good understanding in the sight of God and man. Trust in the Lord with all thine heart; and lean not unto thine own understanding. In all thy ways acknowledge him, and he shall direct thy paths. Prov 3:1-6 (KJV)

MARY HELEN'S TRIAL

128. And I brought him to thy disciples, and they could not cure him. And Jesus answered and said, O faithless and perverse generation, how long shall I be with you? how long shall I bear with you? bring him hither to me. Matt 17:16-17 (ASV)

129. Then came the disciples to Jesus apart, and said, Why could not we cast it out? And he saith unto them, Because of your little faith: for verily I say unto you, If ye have faith as a grain of mustard seed, ye shall say unto this mountain, Remove hence to yonder place; and it shall remove; and nothing shall be impossible unto you. *But this kind goeth not out save by prayer and fasting.* Matt 17:19-21 (ASV)

130. So then faith *cometh* by hearing, and hearing by the word of God. Romans 10:17 (KJV)

131. Vision 2011

132. But as it is written, Eye hath not seen, nor ear heard, neither have entered into the heart of man, the things which God hath prepared for them that love him. But God hath revealed them unto us by his Spirit: for the Spirit searcheth all things, yea, the deep things of God. 1 Corinthians 2:9-10 (KJV)

133. And we know that all things work together for good to them that love God, to them who are the called according to *his* purpose. Romans 8:28 (KJV)

134. And for a spirit of judgment to him that sitteth in judgment, and for strength to them that turn the battle to the gate. Isaiah 28:6 (KJV)

135. Nevertheless the foundation of God standeth sure, having this seal, The Lord knoweth them that are his. And, Let every one that nameth the name of Christ depart from iniquity. 2 Timothy 2:19 (KJV)

136. For the invisible things of him from the creation of the world are clearly seen, being understood by the things that are made, *even* his eternal power and Godhead; so that they are without excuse: Romans 1:20 (KJV)

137. Verily I say unto you, Whosoever shall not receive the kingdom of God as a little child shall in no wise enter therein. Luke 18:17 (KJV)

138. And when they were come to the multitude, there came to him a man, kneeling to him, saying, Lord, have mercy on my son: for he is epileptic, and suffereth grievously; for ofttimes he falleth into the fire, and off-times into the water. And I brought him to thy disciples, and they could not cure him. And Jesus answered and said, O faithless and perverse generation, how long shall I be with you? how long shall I bear with you? bring him hither to me. And Jesus rebuked him; and the demon went out of him: and the boy was cured from that hour. Then came the disciples to Jesus apart, and said, Why could not we cast it out? And he saith unto them, Because of your little faith: for verily I say unto you, If ye have faith as a grain of mustard seed, ye shall say unto this mountain, Remove hence to yonder place; and it shall remove; and nothing shall be impossible unto you. But this kind goeth not out save by prayer and fasting. Matthew 17:14-21 (ASV)

HEY, WHAT'D YOU SAY?

139. "What Are Little Boys Made Of?" is a popular \ (http://en.wikipedia.org/wiki/Nursery rhyme) o "Nursery rhyme" dating from the early nineteenth century. It has a \ (http:// en.wikipedia.org/wiki/Roud Folk Song Index) o "Roud Folk Song Index" number of 821. Iona Archibald Opie (born Iona Archibald, 1923) and Peter Mason Opie (1918–1982) were a husband-and-wife team of \ (http://en.wikipedia.org/wiki/ Folklorist) o "Folklorist", who applied modern techniques to \ (http://en.wikipedia.org/wiki/Children%27s literature) o "Children's literature", summarized in their studies, The Oxford Dictionary of Nursery Rhymes (1951) and The Lore and Language of Schoolchildren (1959). They are also noted \ (http://en.wikipedia.org/wiki/Anthologist) o "Anthologist", and assembled large collections of children's literature, toys and games.

140. WILLIAM MARRION BRANHAM (1909-1965)William Marrion Branham was an influential Bible minister, many thought he was the initiator of healing and charismatic

revivals. From 1947 until his death in 1965, the powerful ministry of William Branham was well known and considered unparalleled in the history of gospel meetings. The impact of the supernatural ministry of this one man was felt not only in North America, but also around the world.

141. Song lyrics: Trust and Obey; John H Sammis [1846-1919] Daniel B Towner [1850-1919]

142. There is no fear in love; but perfect love casteth out fear: because fear hath torment. He that feareth is not made perfect in love. We love him, because he first loved us. 1 John 4:18-19 (KJV)

143. So shalt thou find favour and good understanding in the sight of God and man. **5** Trust in the Lord with all thine heart; and lean not unto thine own understanding. **6** In all thy ways acknowledge him, and he shall direct thy paths. Prov 3:4-6 (KJV)

144. Looking for that blessed hope, and the glorious appearing of the great God and our Saviour Jesus Christ; Who gave himself for us, that he might redeem us from all iniquity, and purify unto himself a peculiar people, zealous of good works. Titus 2:13-14 (KJV)

145. For the Lord himself shall descend from heaven with a shout, with the voice of the archangel, and with the trump of God: and the dead in Christ shall rise first: Then we which are alive and remain shall be caught up together with them in the clouds, to meet the Lord in the air: and so shall we ever be with the Lord. 1 Thessalonians 4:16-17 (KJV) Behold, I shew you a mystery; We shall not all sleep, but we shall all be changed, In a moment, in the twinkling of an eye, at the last trump: for the trumpet shall sound, and the dead shall be raised incorruptible, and we shall be changed. 1 Corinthians 15:51-52 (KJV)

146. And God shall wipe away all tears from their eyes; and there shall be no more death, neither sorrow, nor crying, neither shall there be any more pain: for the former things are passed away. And he that sat upon the throne said, Behold, I make

all things new. And he said unto me, Write: for these words are true and faithful. Revelation 21:4-5 (KJV)

147. My son, forget not my law; but let thine heart keep my commandments: For length of days, and long life, and peace, shall they add to thee. Let not mercy and truth forsake thee: bind them about thy neck; write them upon the table of thine heart: So shalt thou find favour and good understanding in the sight of God and man. Trust in the Lord with all thine heart; and lean not unto thine own understanding. In all thy ways acknowledge him, and he shall direct thy paths. Prov 3:1-6 (KJV)

148. But if ye will not obey the voice of the Lord, but rebel against the commandment of the Lord, then shall the hand of the Lord be against you, as it was against your father. 1 Samuel 12:15 (KJV)

149. Song lyrics: Chorus: The Move Is On; author unknown

THE MOVE IS ON

150. Know ye not that ye are the temple of God, and that the Spirit of God dwelleth in you? If any man defile the temple of God, him shall God destroy; for the temple of God is holy, which temple ye are. 1 Corinthians 3:16-17 (KJV)

151. What? know ye not that your body is the temple of the Holy Ghost which is in you, which ye have of God, and ye are not your own? 1 Corinthians 6:19 (KJV)

152. 152 Idol

   (1.) Heb. aven, "nothingness;" "vanity" [Isaiah 66:3; 41:29; Deuteronomy 32;21; 1 Kings 16:13; Ps 31:6; Jeremiah 8:19].
   (2.) 'Elil, "a thing of naught" [Psalms 97:7; Isaiah 19:3]; a word of contempt, used of the gods of Noph [Ezekiel 30:13].
   (3.) 'Emah, "terror," in allusion to the hideous form of idols [Jeremiah 50:38].
   (4.) Miphletzeth, "a fright;" "horror" [1 Kings 15:13; 2 Chronicles 15:16]

(5.) Bosheth, "shame;" "shameful thing" [Jeremiah 11:13; Hosea 9:10]; as characterizing the obscenity of the worship of Baal.

(6.) Gillulim, also a word of contempt, "dung;" "refuse" ([Ezekiel 16:36; 20:8; Deuteronomy 29:17] marg.).

(7.) Shikkuts, "filth;" "impurity" Ezekiel 37:23; Nahum 3:6].

(8.) Semel, "likeness;" "a carved image" [Deuteronomy 4:16].

(9.) Tselem, "a shadow" [Daniel 3:1; 1 Samuel 6:5], as distinguished from the "likeness," or the exact counterpart.

(10.) Temunah, "similitude" [Deuteronomy 4:12-19]. Here Moses forbids the several forms of Gentile idolatry.

(11.) 'Atsab, "a figure;" from the root "to fashion," "to labour;" denoting that idols are the result of man's labour ([Isaiah 48:5; Psalms 139:24], "wicked way;" literally, as some translate, "way of an idol").

(12.) Tsir, "a form;" "shape" [Isaiah 45:16].

(13.) Matztzebah, a "statue" set up [Jeremiah 43:13]; a memorial stone like that erected by Jacob [Genesis 28:18; 31: 45; 35:14, 20], by Joshua [Genesis 4:9], and by Samuel [1 Samuel 7:12]. It is the name given to the statues of Baal [2 Kings 3:2; 10:27].

(14.) Hammanim, "sun-images." Hamman is a synonym of Baal, the sun-god of the Phoenicians [2 Chronicles 34:4, 7: 14:3, 5; Isaiah 17:8].

(15.) Maskith, "device" [Leviticus 26:1; Numbers 33:52]. In Leviticus 26:1, the words "image of stone" (A.V.) denote "a stone or cippus with the image of an idol, as Baal, Astarte, etc." In Ezekiel 8:12, "chambers of imagery" (maskith), are "chambers of which the walls are painted with the figures of idols;" comp. ver. Ezekiel 10-11.

(16.) Pesel, "a graven" or "carved image" [Isaiah 44:10-20]. It denotes also a figure cast in metal [Deuteronomy 7:25; 27:15; Isaiah 40:19;44:10].

(17.) Massekah, "a molten image" [Deuteronomy 9:12; Judges 17:3-4].

(18.) Teraphim, pl., "images," family gods (penates) worshipped by Abram's kindred [Joshua 24:14]. Put by Michal in David's bed [Judges 17:5; 18:14, 17-18, 20; 1Samuel 19:13 "Nothing can be more instructive and significant than this multiplicity and variety of words designating the instruments and inventions of idolatry." [M.G. Easton; Illustrated Bible Dictionary; 7/22/2011; WordSearch; bible.wordsearchbible.com] Idol An image or anything used as an object of worship in place of the true God. Among the earliest objects of worship, regarded as symbols of deity, were the meteoric stones, which the ancients believed to have been images of the Gods sent down from heaven. From these they transferred their regard to rough unhewn blocks, to stone columns or pillars of wood, in which the divinity worshipped was supposed to dwell, and which were connected, like the sacred stone at Delphi, by being anointed with oil and crowned with wool on solemn days. Of the forms assumed by the idolatrous images we have not many traces in the Bible. Dagon, the fish-god of the Philistines, was a human figure terminating in a fish; and that the Syrian deities were represented in later times in a symbolical human shape we know for certainty. When the process of adorning the image was completed, it was placed in a temple or shrine appointed for it. A Letter of Jeremiah 12:19; Solomon 13:15; 1 Corinthians 8:10. From these temples the idols were sometimes carried in procession, A Letter of Jeremiah 4:26 on festival days. Their priests were maintained from the idol treasury, and feasted upon the meats which were appointed for the idols' use.[William Smith; version 3; Smith's Bible Dictionary; 7/22/2011; WORDsearch Corp; www.wordsearchbible.com]

153. Now the serpent was more subtil than any beast of the field which the Lord God had made. And he said unto the woman,Yea, hath God said, Ye shall not eat of every tree of the garden? And the woman said unto the serpent, We may eat of the fruit of the trees of the garden: But of the fruit of the tree which is in the midst of the garden, God hath said, Ye shall not eat of it, neither shall ye touch it, lest ye die. And the serpent said unto the woman, Ye shall not surely die: Genesis 3:1-4 (KJV)

154. Therefore to him that knoweth to do good, and doeth it not, to him it is sin. James 4:17 (KJV)

155. Therefore to him that knoweth to do good, and doeth it not, to him it is sin. James 4:17 (KJV)

156. Johson Oatman, Jr. & Charles H. Gabriel

157. James Hill

158. Author unknown

159. Virgil Th omson (1896-1989)

ON A QUEST

160. I will instruct thee and teach thee in the way which thou shalt go: I will guide thee with mine eye. Psalms 32:8 (KJV) And the Lord shall guide thee continually, and satisfy thy soul in drought, and make fat thy bones: and thou shalt be like a watered garden, and like a spring of water, whose waters fail not. Isaiah 58:11 (KJV) Howbeit when he, the Spirit of truth, is come, he will guide you into all truth: for he shall not speak of himself; but whatsoever he shall hear, *that* shall he speak: and he will shew you things to come. John 16:13 (KJV)

161. I was glad when they said unto me, Let us go into the house of the Lord. Psalms 122:1 (KJV)

A NEW BEGINNING

162. The original term āåííáù, with its derivatives, may be rendered, (1.) To beget. (2.) To bear or bring forth. (3.) To be begotten. (4.) To be born, or brought forth. 2. Regeneration is, in the Bible, the same as the new birth. 3. To be born again is the same thing, in the Bible use of the term, as to have a new heart, to be a new creature, to pass from death unto life. In other words, to be born again is to have a new moral character, to become holy. To regenerate is to make holy.

> To be born of God … The fact is, the term regeneration, or the being born of God, is designed to express primarily and principally the thing done, that is, the making of a sinner holy, and expresses also the fact, that God's agency induces the change. Throw out the idea of what is done, that is, the change of moral character in the subject, and he would not be born again, he would not be regenerated, and it could not be truly said, in such a case, that God had regenerated him.—Finney's Systematic Theology [Lectures on Systematic Theology; Oberlin College Professor of Theology; Charles G Finney; edited by J H Fairchild; Regeneration – III; 7/22/2011; WORDsearch Corp; www.wordsearchbible.com] And be not conformed to this world: but be ye transformed by the renewing of your mind, that ye may prove what is that good, and acceptable, and perfect, will of God. Romans 12:2 (KJV)

163. [Years later, in the late 1990's, she sent me a message … all her family were saved and serving the Lord because of the change in her that day when she knelt beside a little school desk.]

164. Therefore if any man be in Christ, he is a new creature: old things are passed away; behold, all things are become new. 2 Corinthians 5:17 (KJV)

165. Hast thou not known? hast thou not heard, that the everlasting God, the Lord, the Creator of the ends of the earth, fainteth not, neither is weary? there is no searching of his understanding. He giveth power to the faint; and to them that have no might he increaseth strength. Isaiah 40:28-29 (KJV)

166. And he said unto me, My grace is sufficient for thee: for my strength is made perfect in weakness. Most gladly therefore will I rather glory in my infirmities, that the power of Christ may rest upon me. 2 Cor 12:9 (KJV)

167. And we know that all things work together for good to them that love God, to them who are the called according to *his* purpose. Romans 8:28 (KJV)

168. And God is able to make all grace abound toward you; that ye, always having all sufficiency in all things, may abound to every good work: 2 Corinthians 9:8 (KJV)

169. For then shall be great tribulation, such as was not since the beginning of the world to this time, no, nor ever shall be. And except those days should be shortened, there should no flesh be saved: but for the elect's sake those days shall be shortened. Then if any man shall say unto you, Lo, here is Christ, or there; believe it not. For there shall arise false Christs, and false prophets, and shall shew great signs and wonders; insomuch that, if it were possible, they shall deceive the very elect. Matthew 24:2124 (KJV) But now, O Lord, thou art our father; we are the clay, and thou our potter; and we all are the work of thy hand. Isaiah 64:8 (KJV)

170. I can do all things through Christ which strengtheneth me. Phil 4:13 (KJV)

171. Jesus answered and said unto them, Verily I say unto you, If ye have faith, and doubt not, ye shall not only do this *which is done* to the fig tree, but also if ye shall say unto this mountain, Be thou removed, and be thou cast into the sea; it shall be done. And all things, whatsoever ye shall ask in prayer, believing, ye shall receive. Matt 21:21-22 (KJV)

172. For there is no respect of persons with God. Romans 2:11 (KJV)

173. Jesus Christ the same yesterday, and to day, and for ever. Heb 13:8 (KJV)

SUMMARY

174. Give thanks unto the Lord, call upon his name, make known his deeds among the people. Sing unto him, sing psalms unto him, talk ye of all his wondrous works. Glory ye in his holy name: let the heart of them rejoice that seek the Lord. Seek the

Lord and his strength, seek his face continually. Remember his marvellous works that he hath done, his wonders, and the judgments of his mouth; O ye seed of Israel his servant, ye children of Jacob, his chosen ones. 1 Chronicles 16:8-13 (KJV)Sing unto the Lord, all the earth; shew forth from day to day his salvation. Declare his glory among the heathen; his marvellous works among all nations. For great is the Lord, and greatly to be praised: he also is to be feared above all gods. 1 Chronicles 16:23-25 (KJV)

175. And the Spirit of God came upon Azariah the son of Oded: 2 And he went out to meet Asa, and said unto him, Hear ye me, Asa, and all Judah and Benjamin; The Lord is with you, while ye be with him; and if ye seek him, he will be found of you; but if ye forsake him, he will forsake you. 2 Chronicles 15:1-2 (KJV) But when they in their trouble did turn unto the Lord God of Israel, and sought him, he was found of them. 2 Chronicles 15:4 (KJV) And they entered into a covenant to seek the Lord God of their fathers with all their heart and with all their soul; 2 Chronicles 15:12 (KJV) And they sware unto the Lord with a loud voice, and with shouting, and with trumpets, and with cornets. 15 And all Judah rejoiced at the oath: for they had sworn with all their heart, and sought him with their whole desire; and he was found of them: and the Lord gave them rest round about. 2 Chronicles 15:14-15 (KJV)

176. Seek ye the Lord while he may be found, call ye upon him while he is near: Isaiah 55:6 (KJV)

ABOUT THE AUTHOR

177. I am not worthy of the least of all the mercies, and of all the truth, which thou hast shewed unto thy servant; [for with my staff I passed over this Jordan; and now I am become two bands.] Genesis 32:10 (KJV)

www.ingramcontent.com/pod-product-compliance
Lightning Source LLC
Chambersburg PA
CBHW071429070526
44578CB00001B/43